Treason
on the
Cape Fear

Roots of the Civil War in North Carolina

January — April 1861

Philip Hatfield, PhD

Treason on the Cape Fear

Roots of the Civil War in North Carolina
January – April 1861

Philip Hatfield, PhD

35th Star Publishing
Charleston, West Virginia
www.35thstar.com

Copyright. © 2022 by Philip Hatfield, Ph.D.
All Rights Reserved.
First edition, 2022.
Printed in the United States of America.

No part of this publication may be reproduced, distributed or transmitted in any form or by any means, including photocopying, recording, or other electronic or mechanical methods, without the prior written permission of the publisher, except in the case of brief quotations embodied in critical reviews and certain other noncommercial uses permitted by copyright law.

ISBN-13: 978-1-7378575-5-6
ISBN-10: 1-7378575-5-3

Library of Congress Control Number: 2022935351

35th Star Publishing
Charleston, West Virginia
www.35thstar.com

On the cover:
Colonel John L. P. Cantwell. Private Collection.
2nd Lt. Hanke Vollers, German Volunteers, circa 1860. Courtesy Volley Hanson.
Cape Fear River area map. Library of Congress.
President James Buchanan. Library of Congress.
Governor John W. Ellis. Courtesy North Carolina State Archives.

Cover design and interior layout by: Studio 6 Sense

OTHER CIVIL WAR RELATED BOOKS
BY
PHILIP HATFIELD, PHD

The Rowan Rifle Guards
A History of Company K,
4th North Carolina State Troops, 1857-1861

The Other Feud
The Civil War Service of
William Anderson "Devil Anse" Hatfield

Sacrifice All for the Union
The Civil War Experiences of Captain John Young and His Family
Company G, 13th and 11th West Virginia Volunteer Infantry

The Battle of Hurricane Bridge
With the Firmness of Veterans

AND FORTHCOMING TITLES:

A History of Putnam County, West Virginia
in the Civil War

A History of the 4th West Virginia Volunteer Infantry
Co-authored with Terry Lowry

Available at Amazon and
www.35thstar.com

DEDICATION

*To the loving memory of my parents,
who instilled within me their lifelong love of history.*

*Calvin Lee Hatfield
Freda Jane Hatfield*

Antebellum Wilmington, North Carolina, circa 1853.
Gleason's Pictorial Drawing Room Companion. National Archives.

CONTENTS

Acknowledgments XVII

Introduction XIX

1 – Roots of Division 1

2 – Irreconcilable Differences 25

3 – Antebellum Militia and Volunteer Companies 41

4 – Capture of Fort Caswell and Fort Johnston 55

5 – A Series of Ironic Events 69

6 – Coastal Forts Retaken 77

7 – Soldier Life at Fort Caswell and Fort Johnston in 1861 ... 87

8 – A Time for War 105

Bibliography 115

Notes 123

Name Index 137

About the Author 139

ILLUSTRATIONS

Antebellum Wilmington, North Carolina, circa 1853 IX
Colton's Map of North Carolina, 1861 2
Dred Scott, Leslie's Illustrated, June 27, 1861 4
John Brown's Raid 6
Horrid Massacre in Virginia 7
Wilmington, North Carolina, circa 1847 11
John Brown 13
Enslaved Family, Beaufort, South Carolina, 1862 15
President-elect Abraham Lincoln 17
Winfield Scott 19
South Carolina's Ultimatum 23
Governor John W. Ellis 26
Slave Auction at Richmond, Virginia 29
Lincoln's response to Horace Greeley, Daily National Intelligencer, August 23, 1862 30
President James Buchanan 34
Effects of Fugitive Slave Law 38
North Carolina Militia Officers, 1813 43
Fayetteville Independent Light Infantry, North Carolina Militia, 1834-1853 43
Fayetteville Light Infantry, 1850s 44
Wilmington Light Infantry Armory 44
German Volunteers at Courthouse, circa 1859 46
Lt. Hanke Vollers, German Volunteers 47

Edward P. Chrysostom Cantwell 48

Unidentified militia member from Newbern, Craven County 50

Unidentified member of Gaston Blues 51

Lt. William P. Metts, Newbern Light Infantry 52

2nd Lt. Charles B. Cook, Fayetteville Light Infantry 53

Duplin Rifles, 1859 54

Colonel John L. P. Cantwell 56

Fort Caswell Causeway 58

Colonel John Jackson Hedrick 59

Map of Fort Johnston, 1865 61

Map of Cape Fear River, 1781 64

John B. Floyd 71

Sketch of Fayetteville Arsenal 72

Bombardment of Fort Sumter 78

Interior of Fort Sumter following the attack 79

Lincoln's Call for 75,000 Volunteers 81

Governor John W. Ellis' Response to Lincoln's Call for
75,000 Volunteers 82

Iredell Blues, circa 1860 86

Captain Absalom K. Simonton, Iredell Blues 86

Meshack Franklin Hunt, Rowan Rifle Guards 88

Fort Caswell parade ground 91

Unidentified Rowan Artillery Officer 92

Sketch of Fort Caswell, 1865 94

Coastal Artillery en Barbette 94

Map of Fort Johnston, 1865 100

Pvt. Alfred Turner, 4th NCT 106

Fort Johnston Officers' Quarters, 1900 107
Pvt. William H. Rockwell, 8th NCV, 1861 109
Archibald Daniel Council, Bladen Guards 110
Sketch of Rebel Works on the Cape Fear River, 1865 111
James Isaac Metts, Wilmington Rifle Guards, 1861 112
Unidentified Southern Volunteer, circa 1861 113

ACKNOWLEDGMENTS

The study of history is not an undertaking to be pursued alone. As such, this work would not be possible without the kind assistance of many, including Historian – Author Dr. Chris Fonvielle, and Alison Dineen, Lower Cape Fear Historical Society Archivist, Heather Yenco, Cape Fear Museum, and Fred Taylor, Attorney at Law and avid Civil War image collector, whose expertise proved invaluable. I extend my thanks to image collector Bob Jones, and Elisa Monroe for assisting with editing, and Volley Hanson, descendent of Hanke Vollers, German Volunteers, Paul Weaver, descendent of Franklin Weaver, 4th North Carolina State Troops, and Lamar Williams. Thanks also to Lyric Grimes and the excellent staff at the Wilson Library, Southern Historical Collection, University of North Carolina, Chapel Hill, North Carolina, along with the North Carolina Department of History and Archives. Finally, I would like to thank the North Carolina Baptist Convention for allowing me to view the remains of Fort Caswell.

INTRODUCTION

The series of events culminating in North Carolina's secession on May 20, 1861, was complex, with roots reaching back to the Colonial period. Residents of North Carolina during antebellum shared diverse views on religion, politics, and slavery. By 1860, the underlying social conditions included a large middle class of non-slaveholding whites of modest means, (28% of whites were slave owners) with conservative views on the growth of Federal powers, and strong beliefs in states' rights, similar to those dominating the mindset of early colonial leaders in the state.

Residents evidenced a variety of opinion on every public issue, and in particular showed prejudice toward ideas of movements of outsiders, leading to a strongly isolationistic sense of provincialism as well. Historian William K. Boyd described the state of affairs in his monograph North Carolina on the Eve of Secession,

> In the great drama of 1860-1861 North Carolina had no leading part like that of South Carolina or the far South. The last state except one to ratify the Federal Constitution in 1789, it was also the last one to join the Confederacy. But a study of conditions within its borders on the eve of secession has a value far greater than this relative place in the movement might suggest.
>
> In fact, North Carolina illustrates some phases of Southern life too often lost sight of in discussions of sectional issues. To what extent these conditions existed elsewhere and their place in the history of secession are worthy of inquiry, for Southern society before 1860 did not conform to one type of thought or action. Secession itself was the result of years of conflict on the hustings, the press, and in economic development...the prevailing sentiment was to rebuke the seceders of the south and abolitionists of the North, and to rally in one great effort to save the Union and the Constitution.

As the election approached the motives which shaped the cast of ballots were conflicting. The Whig appeal to the Union and the Constitution found a response in the conservatism of the people and was in line with the trend away from sectional issues to domestic problems.

On the other hand, to defeat Lincoln seemed imperative to preserve the dignity, if not the rights, of the South; and for this duty Breckinridge was undoubtedly the most promising candidate. The results showed a Democratic majority very similar to that in the State election; but the majority of Breckinridge over both Bell and Douglas was only 848 to 4.

Since many Union Democrats cast their votes for Breckinridge as the only hope of defeating Lincoln, his small majority was really a rebuke to the radical State-rights influences which had nominated him. That rebuke to radicalism was repeated in February 1861, when in an election for a convention on Federal relations, the people chose a majority of Union delegates and also voted that the convention should not meet.

Not until President Lincoln's requisition on the State for troops after the firing on Fort Sumter did secession triumph in North Carolina; and then because the only alternative was that of fighting against the South.

Subsequently, after decades of debate over the issue of expanding slavery into the western territories, President James Buchanan was unable to reconcile Northern and Southern states on the matter before leaving office in 1861. Agitated by local and national newspaper conjecture and speculation, North Carolina's coastal residents were fearful of a rumored Federal invasion following Abraham Lincoln's election in November 1860. Their fears piqued on January 9, 1861, when the Federal government chartered a merchant steamer, the Star of the West. While carrying supplies for the Union garrison at Fort Sumter, South Carolina, it attempted to enter Charleston Harbor. It was promptly fired upon and repulsed by shore batteries manned by cadets from the South Carolina Military Academy (later renamed the Citadel).

Afterward, political tensions with the national government heightened across the Southern states, although North Carolina remained steadfastly in the Union. When news of the incident at Charleston Harbor reached Wilmington, however, fear and the desire to protect themselves escalated to a fervor among coastal inhabitants there, many of whom felt North Carolina Governor John W. Ellis was ineffective in dealing with the Federal government.

On January 10, 1861, the City of Wilmington took matters into their own hands and formed a Committee of Safety, and ordered three hundred local militia to capture the United States' Fort Johnston at Smithville, located some thirty miles south of the port city, along with nearby Fort Caswell. The Wilmington militia were joined by another one hundred men from Smithville, and in an unauthorized show of force, they captured the two posts.

Governor Ellis immediately apologized to President Buchanan for the militia taking over the forts. Buchanan was pleased with the apology, but the hasty actions of those excited militiamen proved a significant factor on the road to civil war. Public opinion along the coast rapidly shifted toward secession as many inhabitants there were convinced Ellis was too passive in their protection and insisted on making further preparations for war.

Once sworn into office on March 4, 1861, President Abraham Lincoln told Southerners in his inauguration speech that despite his desire to reconcile, he would "hold, occupy and possess the property and places belonging to the government..." and use force if there was "any show of arms" made to prevent it, alluding to Federal forts and military installations along the Southern coast. Even so, the majority of North Carolinians still opposed secession, yet many coastal residents were leaning toward leaving the Union.

The crisis culminated on April 12, 1861, when South Carolinians attacked Fort Sumter in Charleston Harbor. Lincoln called for 75,000 volunteers to squelch the uprising among Southern states, but Governor Ellis adamantly refused, stating that Lincoln's request was unconstitutional, and sternly replied, "I can be no party to this wicked violation of the laws of the country and to this war upon the liberties of a free people. You can get no troops from North Carolina."

Instead, Ellis ordered the Wilmington militia who took Fort Caswell and Fort Johnston during January 1861 to recapture them on April 19, 1861. This time, however, Ellis offered no apology, and the elated militiamen garrisoned the forts. On April 22, 1861, some four hundred volunteers from Rowan and Cabarrus Counties found themselves on board trains enroute to Fort Caswell and Fort Johnston to support the local militia as a coastal garrison force.

This study therefore examines not only the roots of sectional division in the Old North State, but also focuses on those long forgotten, but tense months of early 1861. *Treason on the Cape Fear* reveals how events on North Carolina's coast demonstrate that the Civil War was already in progress three months prior to the attack on Fort Sumter, challenging the popular narrative that Lincoln initiated the war by calling for 75,000 volunteers.

CHAPTER ONE

ROOTS OF DIVISION

Hostilities in the Civil War did not begin at the attack on Fort Sumter, South Carolina, on April 12, 1861, as popular history suggests. A series of tense events occurred on the southeastern coast of North Carolina in early 1861 when the local militia captured two United States forts on the Cape Fear River, Fort Caswell and Fort Johnston, nearly three months before the attack on Fort Sumter and two months before Abraham Lincoln was inaugurated as the sixteenth President of the United States on March 4, 1861. Tensions leading up to these incidents were deeply rooted in political and sociological conflicts related to slavery that began during the colonial era.

The debate on slavery had gradually intensified for decades, with overt talk of secession emerging among Southern states as early as the 1830's. However, North Carolina generally voiced strong Union sentiments and was known for strong generational links to the old Whig party, which encapsulated the loyalist political tradition of the colonial period. A good example is found in an 1846 pamphlet circulated across the state by Daniel Reaves Goodloe, an abolitionist newspaper editor, who strongly argued against the institution of slavery, asserting that in the long term, a free labor system was more beneficial than slave labor.

However, Goodloe never questioned the moral problem of slavery; rather, he viewed the practice from an economic standpoint, which most conservatives dismissed, typically rebutting that notion by arguing how emancipation would cause a sudden influx of freedmen, causing unfair competition among non-slave holding farmers and other agrarian production sources.[1]

Library of Congress

ROOTS OF DIVISION

The slavery debate persisted, and in 1855, North Carolina enacted a new law, entitled, "Slaves and Free Persons of Color. An Act Concerning Slaves and Free Persons of Color," *North Carolina Revised Code No. 105*. This bill stated,

> Any inhabitant of this State desirous to emancipate any slave or slaves, shall file a petition...setting forth, as near as may be, the name, sex, and age of each slave intended to be emancipated, and praying permission to emancipate the same; and the court before whom such petition shall be filed, shall grant the prayer thereof on the following conditions, and not otherwise, viz.
>
> That the petitioner shall shew that he has given public notice of his intention to file such petition at the court house of the county, and in the State Gazette, for at least six weeks before the hearing of such petition; and that the petitioner shall enter into bond with two securities, each to be good and sufficient, payable to the State of North Carolina, in the sum of one thousand dollars for each slave named in the petition, conditioned that the said slave or slaves shall honestly and correctly demean him, her or themselves, while he, she or they shall remain within the State of North Carolina, and that he, she or they will, within ninety days after granting the prayer of the petitioner to emancipate him, her or them, leave the State of North Carolina, and never afterwards come within the same: *Provided nevertheless*, That no such emancipation shall in any manner whatever invalidate or affect the rights or claims of any creditor of such petitioner.[2]

One year later, the fledgling Republican Party nominated the well-known explorer, John C. Fremont, as the first candidate to openly oppose the institution of slavery. The Republican Party platform focused on preventing the extension of slavery into the western territories, yet it did not seek emancipation across the nation. Despite this, Southern Democrats balked, believing that if a Republican became president, they would quickly abolish slavery and destroy their economy. As such, the Republican Party had few Southern supporters, with their largest base of support found in Northern states.[3]

In opposition, former Secretary of State and Pennsylvania attorney, James Buchanan, won the Democratic party nomination for President that year. His platform was based on the popular state sovereignty notion to expand slavery into the western territories, emphasizing that Congress did not possess the Constitutional power to interfere with the states and territories as to how the practice of slavery was regulated. Acquiring the popular support in both southern and western states, Buchanan won the 1856 election.[4]

Library of Congress

When The Supreme Court of the United States released the Dred Scott decision in 1857, it ostensibly settled the question of whether the

Federal government could impede the expansion of slavery into the western territories. The court ruled the Missouri Compromise unconstitutional, stating that slaves were not citizens of the United States, and therefore without rights. The decision was eventually rendered moot by the Fourteenth Amendment in 1868, which guaranteed citizenship to anyone born or naturalized in the United States. A summary of the Dred Scott decision appeared in the *Raleigh Standard* on March 11, 1857,

> ...this is the most important decision ever made by any Court in this country, and that it fortifies as by a wall of brass the rights of the slaveholder in the States and in the common territories. Congress, it is expressly declared, has no constitutional power to prohibit slavery in the territories; and possessing no such power, cannot delegate it to a territorial government.
>
> No territorial government can, therefore, abolish slavery. If the "legal condition of the slave is not affected by his sojourn in another State," surely it cannot be affected by his removal to a territory; and if Congress possesses no power over slavery in the territories, surely no portion of the inhabitants of a territory can constitutionally declare that another portion shall not be secure in the rights which they enjoyed when in sovereign States, and which they have carried with them to the common territories of the Union.
>
> The idea of the abolitionists, that a slave is free as soon as he touches the soil of a free State, is again exploded; for it is declared that he remains a slave, though sojourning in a free State, and the right of his owner to his body and to his services cannot be affected...[5]

Despite Buchanan's hope that the Dred Scott decision would calm the escalating sectionalist tensions over the issue of slavery, the opposite occurred. On October 16-18, 1859, a group of twenty-one men, including four former slaves and a free black man from Canada, led by John Brown of Connecticut, captured the United States arsenal at Harper's Ferry, Virginia, hoping to spark a slave rebellion in the Southern states.

United States Secretary of War, John B. Floyd of Virginia, had received "anonymous" intelligence warning the government that the Federal arsenal would be attacked on or about October 15, 1859, but the threat was not taken seriously, and Brown became a martyr among abolitionists when he was hung at Charles Town, Virginia, on December 2, 1859.⁶

John Brown's Raid. Library of Congress.

This incident increased anxieties in Southern states, including North Carolina, with fears of an insurrection again dominating the newspapers similar to the aftermath of the Nat Turner Rebellion in 1831, when a group of slaves murdered between fifty-five and sixty-five people, at least fifty-one of whom were white.⁷

Newspapers in coastal North Carolina blamed the Northern editors and abolitionists for the recent events at Harper's Ferry, describing John Brown's raid as an insurrection, rebellion, and treason. The *Wilmington Journal* opined on October 21, 1859,

> Of the very incendiary and treasonous outbreak which the telegraph on yesterday announced to us as having transpired at Harper's Ferry, Va., much might be said in a certain direction, but with greater propriety, just at this present time, might be

left unsaid. But as to the probable result in the political world, though nothing definite or satisfactory can be elicited now, yet we apprehend that it's influence will be more than positively felt in the next presidential campaign.

HORRID MASSACRE IN VIRGINIA.

Library of Congress.

Its influence is pregnant with good or evil to the country and will be positive and not negative in its actions. In our opinion the election or defeat of the Charleston nominee [*sic* - southern Democrat candidate] can readily be traced to Harper's Ferry... and in a very great measure depends upon the impression made upon the mind of the northern public on the reception of the news yesterday.

Of the causes which led to this unheard-of exhibition of puerile fanaticism, speculation is rife, and their disclosure must be left to time. We suppose that the rioters, if not already killed by an excited populace, will soon take part in a hemp stretching, or gander pulling, perhaps the latter is more the appropriate term. Whether the punishment be for treason in attacking the government armory, or for violating the laws of Virginia, the result will be much the same – hemp will certainly be stretched, and never in a more righteous cause; to this end we desist from saying more, and perhaps the less said about it, the better for all concerned.[8]

A week later on October 28, 1859, the editor of the *Wilmington Journal* again opined on the effects of John Brown's raid and used the occasion to present another duplicitous attempt to blame Northern abolitionist editors for biasing readers against slavery, while simultaneously inserting a not-so-subtle pitch for the notion of benevolent slavery as the reason the raid failed to incite a slave rebellion. Clearly, other period evidence contradicts such arguments that slavery was altruistic, although some slaves later recalled experiencing much less harsh treatment in Wilmington.

One such person was John H. Jackson. Born into slavery at Wilmington in 1851, Jackson worked in the home of a wealthy family. At the time, New Hanover County was the largest city in North Carolina, and enslaved men, women, and children comprised around half of the county's population. In a 1932 interview, Jackson shared his recollections of life in bondage. When asked about whether slave holders there were abusive, he recalled,

> Mos' all the fine work around Wilmington was done by slaves…they called 'em artisans… We had a lot of them artisans among our folks. They all lived on our place with they families. They hired themselves when they pleased, they colle'ted they pay, an' the onliest thing the owner took was enough to support they families."
>
> "Did I ever know of any slaves bein' whipped? I seen plenty of 'em whipped over at the jail, but…they needed whippin'. But (with a chuckle) I sho' would have hated to see anybody put they han's on one of my owner's people. We was all 'spectable and did'n know nothin' about whippen…
>
> I believe we was all happy as slaves because we had the best of kare (care). I don't believe none of us was sold off because I never heard tell of it. I have always served nice folks and never associated with any other kind…I don't know nothing about field han's and workmen on the river, but so far as I knows, the carpenters and people like that started work at 8 o'clock A.M. and stopped at 5 o'clock P.M. Of course, 'round the house it was different. Our folks done pretty much what the white folks did because we was all pretty much one an' other."[9]

Another former slave from Wilmington, eighty-three-year old Isabell Henderson, lived in a large house near the Jewish Synagogue on Market Street, which she referred to as the "Clock Church" because it had a large clock on the front of the building. She recalled,

> ...I was jus' five years old when the men went away. I guess to the war I don' know. Some men come by and conscrip'd dem. I don't know where they went but I guess to war. I was such a little girl I don't 'member much. But I does know my missus was good to me. I used to play with her little boy. I was jes one of the family. I played with the little boy around the house 'cause I was never 'lowed to run the streets. They was good to us. They kept me in clothes, pretty clothes....Yes'm we was slaves but we had good times.[10]

Generally, slaves living with wealthier families in Wilmington appear to have received better treatment than those in more agrarian environments, although in reality it was still life in bondage. As far as participating in a rebellion, however, most were terrified to do so, as taking part of such dissent would have likely led to the gallows or other severe punishment.

One coastal resident wrote,

> ...Their actions had all the effects of a surprise-no one could calculate their force, and no one dreamed that a handful of men not exceeding at any time fifty, would have dared undertaken such an enterprise as old Brown and his crowd did. In this connection, we may remark that recently there has been a great clamor for civil and against military superintendence, even where the character of the works carried is decidedly military. Had there been a proper military element in the superintendency at Harper's Ferry, the result would have been different, no doubt.
>
> The insurgents were disappointed in the presumed readiness of the slaves to join them. That is one consideration calculated to strike reasoning men in the north, no matter what their abstract ideas on the subject of slavery may be; for it shows them that the stories they have heard existing between master and slave in the

South are wholly erroneous-that is, there is neither oppression on the one hand, nor antagonism on the other.

Another aspect of the case, and one that ought to be well pondered, is that nearly all these emissaries, Brown, Cook, etc., had been connected with Kansas shrieking and Kansas outrage-have been aided and abetted by Gerritt Smith, Henry Ward Beecher, Horace Greeley, etc. Have in their hands the Sharpe's rifles got up for service against the rights of southern people going to that territory...

Again, we are fully warned of the fact that the Abolitionists of the north will stop not with stealing and political robbery-they would resort to actual violence on our own soil; that is, they would urge on such tools as old Brown, but be precious careful not to expose their own valuable lives. Finally, it shows us that we require what we never yet had – a volunteer *system*. We have plenty of volunteers, or at least of men willing to volunteer in an emergency, but these are isolated....We want a *system*.

We are not inclined to be alarmists, but we may rest assured that precautions cannot be misplaced, for our own protection, but even more for the protection of the slave; for while the result of any attempted movement, no sane man could entertain a moment's doubt, it is difficult to estimate the evils which might flow from the efforts of fanaticism and desperation, if allowed to be exerted for even the shortest time.[11]

As word of the raid on Harper's Ferry saturated the nation, pro-slavery advocates similarly sought to bolster their case using particulars of the raid. Many newspapers erroneously claimed Brown was unable to recruit any blacks to aid in the attack on the arsenal; while he attempted to persuade Harriet Tubman, who declined due to illness, and Frederick Douglass, who also refused, thinking Brown's plan was not only a "suicide mission," but also an attack on the Federal government. He responded that such a move would, "...array the whole country against us" and warned Brown, "You will never get out alive."[12]

Another example is found in an article entitled, "A Misnomer" published in the *Wilmington Daily Herald*, on October 26, 1859. The writer deliberately avoided calling the raid an insurrection, hoping to minimize the role the former slaves played in the attack, by attempting to paint another picture of benevolent, albeit paternalized slavery. It should be noted there were indeed cases of close relations between slaves and their owners during this era, but available evidence indicates it was less common than the Southern press usually sought to make it appear.

Wilmington, North Carolina, circa 1847. Courtesy Amon Carter Museum.

The following editorial further illustrates the influence newspaper editors had on escalating sectionalist tensions,

> Why will Editors persist in calling the late affair at Harper's Ferry an "Insurrection?" We have several papers before us published in the State and out of it – and they nearly all of them allude to it as being an insurrection among the negroes. 'Twas no insurrection, and it is a libel upon the slave in designating it as such. They had nothing whatever to do with it. *There was not a single slave engaged but what was drawn in by compulsion.*
>
> The original insurgents consisted of some fifteen or sixteen *white* men and a half dozen *free negroes* from the North, brought there by old Brown. What few slaves engaged in the affair were forced into taking up arms *after* the original outbreak, through *fear* of white abolitionists, and *not* from love of them, or hatred towards their masters. They did not want to join the insurgents. They hesitated, preferring slavery in the South to freedom – or such freedom as they knew they would get at the hands of old Brown and his devilish crew at the North. We really think the slaves about Harper›s Ferry deserve credit for the manner in which they behaved in this treasonable affair.
>
> What was easier than for them to seize arms – for there were any quantity of them on hand – rush upon their masters in the dead of night and slay whole families before a step could be taken to prevent the dreadful work. When the deed was done, what easier than to quickly tramp over into Pennsylvania, only a few miles distant, and bury themselves among the abolitionists, where it would be next to impossibility to discover them. These things could have been done easily, but witness how nobly the "poor old slaves," – as they are called by their would-be friends, but in reality, their worst enemies, – did.
>
> They refused to take up arms against their masters – the only friends they knew – and not until forced into by threats of death, was it done, and then only a few, comparatively speaking, joined the blood-thirsty, demented fanatics of the North in their treasonable work. Of course, as long as we down South continue to call the late affair an Insurrection, just so long will we be playing into the hands of Northern fanatics.

They want it put in that light. It strengthens their doctrine, of course. If they can make it appear that the slaves are dissatisfied with their mode of life, and are desirous of changing it, even at the expense of blood, a great point with them is gained. They then have – according to their incendiary belief – an excuse for invading Southern territory.

John Brown. Library of Congress.

They say the slaves are desirous – aye, even anxious, to throw off the yoke of servitude; and shall we stand idly by and not help our fellow creatures in their hour of need? Thus, they reason, and as long as we continue to insist upon calling a fool-hardy invasion of white men and free negroes an insurrection, just so long will we continue to strengthen the cause of our enemies.

Divest the thing of the insurrectionary aspect, and what do we behold? The foundation of their whole doctrine overthrown. – The negroes do not desire freedom. They had an opportunity – a good one. Months were wasted in consummating the arrangements and yet when the blow was to be struck and freedom granted, – the great boon which those wild, deluded fanatics of the North and North-West prate so much about – where do we find the poor slave? Why quietly sitting at home by his master's fire side, or doing his master's bidding, while a dozen or more crazy fools are battling for *his* rights which he will not accept.

We are surprised that Southern papers should call this invasion of a few treasonable men upon the South an insurrection, when not the first feature of it assumes that aspect. We say desist from it. It is exactly what the abolitionists want…and we almost feel rejoiced that this thing has happened, for it has taught us two things, first that we can put confidence in the fidelity of the blacks as a mass…and secondly it has taught northern fanatics that in future if they desire to liberate the slaves from bondage they must resort to other means, for this thing has taught them that expecting aid and comfort from the slaves themselves is putting faith in a broken reed…

We don't know of any little event connected with this affair which has pleased us more than this reluctance of the slaves to engage in the dirty work. Not even the capture of old Brown himself can equal the pleasure we experience when thinking about it. To old Brown it must be the unkindest cut of all…when the Sheriff cuts the rope which is to rob him of his worthless life.[13]

The strength of nationalist sentiment became painfully obvious to the Southern states when Abraham Lincoln received 180 out of 303 electoral votes with only forty percent of the popular vote in the November 1860 election. This incensed neighboring South Carolina and Virginia, yet secessionists remained a minority in North Carolina. Nonetheless, citizens in the southeastern coastal areas of North Carolina felt particularly threatened in December 1860 when President James Buchanan announced his resolve to protect the United States' forts located along the southeastern coast, including those in North Carolina. Knowing his constituency was growing restless, North Carolina Governor John W. Ellis, then in his first term of office, wrote to Secretary of War John B. Floyd, on December 10, 1859, requesting more arms for the state militia,

The sense of insecurity prevailing among the people of this state, renders it necessary that I should apply to you for arms to place in the hands of the militia. I wish to procure from the Government, two thousand long range rifles with bayonets attached for the use of the State of North Carolina. If these arms cannot be furnished, I would be glad to have an advance made, to be deducted from the quotas of arms that will become due to this State in the next and Seceding years....[14]

Enslaved family, Beaufort, South Carolina, 1862. Library of Congress

As talk of secession persisted, former Whig turned Democrat, North Carolina Senator Zebulon Baird Vance (1830-1894) and future wartime governor (and a strong unionist) was deeply concerned about the possibility of secession. Vance astutely perceived the public was being manipulated into a heightened state of anxiety and fear, which could lead to a hasty decision with irrevocable and devastating consequences for the South. He wrote to his friend, William Dickson, December 11, 1860,

> The Whole Southern mind is inflamed to the highest pitch and the leaders in the disunion move are scorning every suggestion of compromise and rushing everything with ruinous and indecent haste that would seem to imply that they were absolute fools. Yet they are acting wisely for their ends; they are precipitating the people into a revolution without giving them time to think.
>
> They fear lest the people shall think. But the people must think, and when they do begin to think and hear the matter properly discussed they will consider long and soberly before they tear down this noble fabric and invite anarchy and confusion, carnage, civil war, and financial ruin with the breathless hurry of men flying from pestilence.
>
> If we go out now, we can't take the army and the navy with us, and Lincoln could as easily employ them to force us back as he could to prevent our going out. We have everything to gain and nothing on earth to lose by delay, but by too hasty action we may take a fatal step that we never can retrace, we may lose a heritage that we can never recover though we seek it earnestly and with tears.[15]

Leading residents of Craven County, North Carolina, were equally concerned. Organizing a large gathering of residents, they met on December 12, 1860, to discuss "the present alarming state of national affairs." The citizens asserted that white North Carolinians possessed a "common interest with slaveholding states" since the state had "suffered from the aggressions of the North upon the institution of slavery until the burden has become intolerable."[16]

Despite being aware of the Dred Scott decision, the group resolved to seek new constitutional protections against the Northern states to stop passing laws "hostile to slavery" although the majority were also still strongly pro-Union and could not agree on the constitutionality of secession. They further admonished Governor John Ellis to organize a convention and immediately bolster and reorganize the militia, which had been in disarray for years.[17]

Many militia companies around the state were already in progress of preparing for war, however. Captain Joseph Todd, 95th Regiment North

Carolina Militia, wrote to Governor Ellis on December 15, 1859, petitioning to have more officers commissioned to aid in better organizing the regiment,

> I wish you if it is consistent with the public service, to send me some 25 or 30 commissions for officers of the militia of the 95th regiment of N. Carolina as I have none, and but very few officers commissioned. The times look a little squally, and I would like to have my Boys in good trim if they should be needed...[18]

President-elect Abraham Lincoln, 1860. Library of Congress.

Throughout 1860 Southern states continued to debate secession, largely motivated by concerns that Abraham Lincoln would be elected. South Carolina Governor William H. Gist wrote to Governor John Ellis on October 6, 1860, expressing anxiety over events transpiring across the nation, and because of the probability of Lincoln's election, he encouraged Ellis to join in moving his state toward a convention to discuss secession. Ellis responded on October 19, 1860,

> In compliance with your request, I will give as accurately as I my power to do, an account of the views and feelings of the people of North Carolina upon the important subject of your communication. Political differences and party stripe have been so high in this state for some years past, and particularly during the past nine months that anything like unanimity upon a public question could scarcely be expected; and luck is the call with the one under consideration. Our people are very far from being agreed as to which action the state should take in the event of Lincoln's election to the presidency.
>
> Some favor subdivisions, some resistance, and others still would await the course of events that may follow. Many argue that he would be powerless for evil with a minority in the Senate and perhaps in the House of Representatives also; while others say, and doubtless with certain sincerity, that the placing of the powers of the Federal government into his hands would prove a fatal blow to the institution of negro slavery in this country.
>
> None of our public speakers, I believe, have taken the ground before the people, that the election of Lincoln of itself, would, be a cause of secession. Many have said it would not, while others have spoken equivocally. Upon the whole, I am decidedly of the opinion that a majority of our people would consider the occurrence of the event referred to as sufficient ground for dissolving the union of the states. For which reason I do not suppose that our legislature, which will meet on the 19th prox., will take any steps in that direction: Such for instance, as the calling of a convention.
>
> Thus Sir, I have given you what I conceive to be the sentiment of our people upon the subject of your letter, and I give it as an

existing fact, without comment as to whether the majority be in error or not. My own opinions as an individual are of but little monument. It will be sufficient to say, that as a States Rights man, believing in the sovereignty and ____ powers of the state, I will conform my actions to the action of North Carolina whatever that may be.

To this general observation, I will make but a single qualification. It is this, I could not, in any event, assent to, or give my aid to a practical enforcement of the monstrous doctrine of coercion. I do not for a moment think that North Carolina would become a party to the enforcement of this doctrine and will not, therefore, do her the injustice of placing her in that position, even though hypothetically.[19]

General Winfield Scott. Library of Congress.

Lieutenant General Winfield Scott, hero of the Mexican War, was the commander of United States military forces in 1860. On December 15, 1860, Scott advised President James Buchanan that the Federal forts located in principle Southern states were vulnerable to takeover by hostile citizens, that with talk of secession looming over the nation, they should be on alert for surprise attacks, particularly Fort Sumter in South Carolina, along with Forts Jackson, St. Phillipe, Morgan, Pulaski, Pickens and McRee.[20]

Additionally, the Pensacola, Florida, Navy yard was also placed on alert. Scott stated, "…as there was not a soldier in Ft Sumpter, any handful of secessionists might seize and occupy it, &c. &c." Buchanan disagreed with the risk, contending such action would be construed as hostile and could potentially trigger the Southern states into war. Rather, the president wanted to evacuate Fort Sumter, instead of reinforcing the garrison.[21]

Not surprisingly, his Secretary of War, John B. Floyd, also disagreed. Floyd was all the while covertly moving a large cache of government firearms to Southern arsenals in anticipation of civil war. Scott later recalled attempting to persuade Buchanan to act, "…that I might make one effort more to save the forts and the Union."[22]

At this point, South Carolina was on the verge of seceding, but had not yet done so. Scott wrote,

> There being, at the moment, no danger of an early secession beyond So. Carolina, the president in reply to my arguments for immediately reinforcing Fort Moultrie and sending a garrison to Fort Sumter, said, "the time has not arrived for doing so; that, a commission would be appointed and sent to negotiate…respecting the secession of the state & the property of the U.S. held within its limits; and that if Congress should decide against the secession, then he would send a reinforcement, and telegraph the commanding officer (Major Anderson) of Fort Moultrie, to 'hold the forts (Moultrie and Sumpter) against attack.'
>
> …Long prior to the Force bill March 2, 1833, prior to the issue of his proclamation, and in part prior to the passage of the Ordnance of Nullification – President Jackson, under the Act of March 3, 1807, authorizing the employment of the land and

naval forces, caused reinforcements to be sent to Fort Moultrie & a sloop of war (the *Natchez*) with two revenue cutters, to be sent to Charleston Harbor in order to,

1. Prevent seizure of the fort, and
2. To enforce the execution of revenue laws. Genl. Scott, himself, arrived at Charleston the day after passage of the Ordnance of Nullification, and many of the additional companies were then in route for the same destination. President Jackson familiarly said, at the time that, by the assemblage of those forces, for lawful purposes, he was not making war upon So. Carolina, but if So. Carolina attacked them, it would be So. Carolina that made war upon the United States.

...further ask the attention of the Secretary to Forts Jefferson and Taylor, which are wholly national, being of far greater value even to the most distant points of the Atlantic Coast and the people on the upper waters of the Missouri, Mississippi, and Ohio rivers, than to the state of Florida. There is only a feeble company at Key West for the defence of Fort Taylor, and not a solider in Fort Jefferson to resist a handful of filibusters or rowboat of pirates; & the gulf soon after the beginning of secession, or revolutionary troubles, in the adjacent states, will swarm with such nuisances.[23]

Amidst rising tensions, several North Carolina counties held public meetings to discuss ways to counteract what they perceived as attempts by radical abolitionists of the North to subjugate the South. One such committee in Sampson County adopted a resolution calling for a commercial embargo against the North and called for the death penalty for any citizen found circulating "incendiary" publications that could incite another slave revolt such as occurred in Virginia in 1831 during the Nat Turner Rebellion.[24]

Following the 1860 presidential elections, on November 28, 1860, Governor John Ellis wrote candidly in his diary that several North Carolina counties were holding public meetings discussing the question of secession, including Samson, McDowell, Wilson, Cumberland, Halifax, and Edgecombe, and noted they were expressing "the strongest southern feelings." The next day Ellis diarized that the situation in South Carolina appeared that secession was imminent, and that "This for everything looks as though the Union is on the verge of dissolution."[25]

Yet, a significant population of North Carolina still held Union sentiments. For example, the citizens of Whiteville, (located about fifty miles from Wilmington) met on December 21, 1860, just one day after South Carolina seceded. During the meeting, city leader John Meares made a compelling case to remain loyal to the Union. His oration caused community leaders to establish resolutions to preserve the Union and to settle the differences with the North peaceably without secession.[26]

Also in December 1860, a bill attempting to accomplish such a settlement was proposed in the United States Congress known as the *Crittenden Compromise*. That bill was suggested by a Senator from Kentucky on December 18, 1860. It would have enabled a series of Constitutional amendments allowing Southern states to maintain rights to slavery without Federal interference and allowed any new territories or states afterward to decide the matter on their own without Federal regulation, but likewise condemned the practice as illegal in Northern states.[27]

On December 20, 1860, South Carolina seceded. Calls for secession then spread rapidly across the South, although the North Carolina legislature remained steadfast in favor of remaining in the Union. Other states, such as Alabama and Mississippi, now demanded that the North must concede to slavery in the territories, or the South would leave the Union, as sectional differences were irreconcilable.

Secretary of War John B. Floyd resigned on December 29, 1860, amidst a scandal over his unscrupulous dealings with Indian Bonds. The next day, General Winfield Scott again attempted to persuade President Buchanan and Floyd's replacement, Secretary of War John Holt, a former Army Advocate General who was strongly opposed to secession, to reinforce the garrison at Fort Sumter.

General Scott hastily penned a letter requesting permission to go around the War Department,

> ...matters of the highest national importance seem to forbid a moments delay...Will the President permit Genl. S. without reference to the War Department, & otherwise as secretly as

possible, to send two hundred and fifty recruits from New York Harbor to reinforce Fort Sumter, together with some extra muskets or rifles, ammunition, and sustenance? It is hoped that a sloop of war and cutter may be ordered for the same purpose, as early as tomorrow. Genl. S. will wait upon the President at any moment he may be called for. The So. Carolina commission had already been many days in Washington, with no movements of defence (on part of the U.S.) was permitted.[28]

Library of Congress.

Obviously frustrated, Scott later openly blamed Buchanan's passivity; although the embattled president clarified that his intention was to make every last minute effort possible to preserve the Union and avoid a civil war. Scott was at wits end, and likely due to his extensive military command experience, could foresee the impending political decision matrix ending in hostilities,

It would have been easy to reinforce this fort down to about the 12th of February…the late President refused to allow any attempt to be made because he was holding negotiations with the So. Carolina commissioners. Afterward, Secretary Holt and myself endeavored, in vain, to obtain a ship of war for the purpose & finally were obliged to employ the passenger steamer, *Star of the West*. That vessel, but for the hesitation of the master, might, as is generally believed, have delivered, at the fort, the men and sustenance on board.

This attempt at succor failing, I next, verbally, submitted to the late cabinet either that succor be sent by ships of war, fighting their way by the batteries (increasing in strength daily) or that Major Anderson should be left to ameliorate his condition by the muzzles of his guns; that is, enforcing his supplies by bombardment, & by bringing to merchant vessels, helping himself (giving orders for payment) or finally, be allowed to evacuate the fort, which, in that case, would be inevitable. But before any resolution was taken, - the late Secretary of the Navy, making difficulties about the want of suitable war vessels - another commissioner from So. Carolina arrived, causing further delay.[29]

CHAPTER TWO

IRRECONCILABLE DIFFERENCES

On January 1, 1861, North Carolina Governor John W. Ellis was only recently re-elected to a second term as the thirty-fifth governor of the Old North State. Raised on his father's plantation in the eastern part of Rowan County, in the area that later became Davidson County, he lacked a penchant for farming and attended Randolph Macon College and the University of North Carolina at Chapel Hill. Ellis later studied law under Richard M. Pearson in Mocksville, North Carolina, and was admitted to the Rowan County Bar in 1842. In 1844, Ellis began his political career when he was elected to the North Carolina House of Commons.[30]

A strong Democrat from a largely Whig county, Ellis was decidedly loyal to the Union, but when South Carolina seceded from the Union on December 20, 1860, Ellis was deeply concerned that the country was rapidly escalating toward a civil war. Only a few days earlier, on January 3, 1861, militia from Savannah, Georgia, seized Fort Pulaski.

On the same date, the state of Delaware voted not to secede from the Union. As the crisis escalated, Alabama Governor A.B. Moore ordered the state militia to seize Fort Gaines, Fort Morgan, and the U.S. Arsenal at Mount Vernon on January 4, 1861. They had all those Federal installations under state control by January 5, 1861. Florida militia likewise responded by seizing all the Federal forts located along its coast on January 6, 1861.

Governor John W. Ellis. Courtesy North Carolina State Archives.

The *Fayetteville Observer*, an anti-secession news organ, reported on January 7, 1861, in an article entitled "The Secession Flag at Wilmington" the growing secession sentiment at a recent public meeting,

> Among the speeches noted...argued that a seceding State has a right to take the forts and other government property within its limits or on its coast; and that the present Union was based on the principle of secession, insomuch as the nine States which adopted the Constitution had seceded from the old confederation, and set up a new government, leaving North Carolina to come in or stay out as she liked.
> In our opinion, a State has as much right to take the forts as it has to secede - no more and no less – simply the right of

revolution. There could scarcely be a more preposterous claim than this, that after the United States had bought from South Carolina and improved it an immense expense, South Carolina should have a right to take it back, without the consent of the United States.

As to the old Confederation, the states had found the agreement, originally made, called a Confederation, totally inefficient, they all admitted this, and they all met together in convention under the call of Congress to make a new agreement to form a more perfect Union. There was no secession, or anything like secession, by one state or by nine states, the same process may be gone through with now, this difference: that whereas each State then had the right to ratify or reject and be in or out as it chose. Now a ratification of a change by three-fourths is binding upon the whole.[31]

Also on January 7, 1861, the North Carolina General Assembly submitted four resolutions to the Senate, ironically just three days prior to the takeover of Forts Caswell and Johnston on the Cape Fear River, south of Wilmington. Three of the resolutions related to holding a convention dealing with the question of secession and expressed the House's intent to remain in the Union. However, it also posited,

> ...unless by the 4th day of March next the lust of exclusive Northern sectional domination shall be quenched and a reaction in public sentiment at the North upon the subject of slavery shall have taken place...it will be the duty of North Carolina, making common cause with her sister states of the South to seek her safety out of the Union.

Resolution three stated,

> Resolved that the Governor be requested to inform the Senate if any portion of the citizens of North Carolina have consulted with him upon the propriety of taking possession of the United States forts in North Carolina or any one of others.
>
> What propositions were made and by whom and what was his advice and reply. And if he is advised of any plan by which the forts of the United States in North Carolina are to be occupied

on or before the 4th of March next by any authority or force other than that of the United States.³²

Political relationships with the United States were strained across the South, and Governor John Ellis was acutely aware of the growing tension in the state's coastal region, where the shipping and slave sales produced significant revenue. During the decades prior to 1860, North Carolina achieved significant economic growth from the slave auctions, along with exporting cotton and other products to the North and Europe.

Slavery became especially lucrative when the newly opened western territories saw increased migration rates, as emerging entrepreneurs frequently purchased slaves from southeastern North Carolina prior to moving to the western territories. Many slave dealers, known as Speculators, also came from the lower south to purchase slaves at auctions in North Carolina. The rush to acquire new lands in territories such as Missouri and Texas between 1810 and 1860 resulted in an estimated 140,000 slaves either sold or transported out of North Carolina.³³

Representative T. N. Crumpler of Ashe County clearly recognized the threat to North Carolina's slave trade that secession would present, and in a speech given to the House of Commons on Federal Relations in early January 1861, revealed a poignant picture of the conflicted nature of affairs at that time.

He illustrated not only how the newspapers created rumors, and subsequently played key roles in escalating sectionalist tensions, but also evidenced an inherently contradictory desire to remain in the Union while preserving slavery, all while blaming the radical abolitionists and South Carolina.

Strongly Union, Crumpler's desire to preserve the institution of slavery within the Union will seem morally irreprehensible to the modern reader; however, in that era, such was not anomalous. Despite certain popular myths, four slave states also remained in the Union when the war began, including Delaware, Kentucky, Maryland and Missouri. Further, when West Virginia was admitted into the Union on June 20, 1863, the new state government allowed slavery to continue until 1865. Crumpler opined,

IRRECONCILABLE DIFFERENCES

...Already the disruption of the Government is begun. One State has declared herself out of the Union; others are threatening to make the same declaration. Even while I stand here speaking, they may have consummated their secession ordinances. A revolution seems to have commenced, and, as yet no effectual barrier to its progress has been erected. In North Carolina, the same spirit which prompted the hasty action of those who have inaugurated this revolution is at work...

Slave Auction at Richmond, Virginia. Library of Congress.

...Conceiving that some better excuse for disunion than any which had yet arisen must be made before they could hope to arouse the passions of the Southern people and bind them to their policy, they set to work to bring that excuse into existence. They had, before this, declared that the election of any Republican to the Presidency would furnish a sufficient cause for a dissolution of the Union.

...There is another class–the Abolitionists of the North–who are primarily responsible and most guilty in this matter. With hearts full of treason to the spirit of the Constitution, they have, for years, been digging at the foundation of our government.

WASHINGTON.

"LIBERTY AND UNION, NOW AND FOREVER, ONE AND INSEPARABLE."

SATURDAY, AUGUST 23, 1862.

A LETTER FROM THE PRESIDENT.

EXECUTIVE MANSION,
Washington, August 22, 1862.

Hon. HORACE GREELEY:

DEAR SIR: I have just read yours of the 19th, addressed to myself through the New York Tribune. If there be in it any statements, or assumptions of fact, which I may know to be erroneous, I do not now and here controvert them. If there be in it any inferences which I may believe to be falsely drawn, I do not now and here argue against them. If there be perceptible in it an impatient and dictatorial tone, I waive it in deference to an old friend whose heart I have always supposed to be right.

As to the policy I "seem to be pursuing," as you say, I have not meant to leave any one in doubt.

I would save the Union. I would save it the shortest way under the Constitution. The sooner the national authority can be restored the nearer the Union will be "the Union as it was." If there be those who would not save the Union unless they could at the same time *save* slavery, I do not agree with them. If there be those who would not save the Union unless they could at the same time *destroy* slavery, I do not agree with them. My paramount object in this struggle *is* to save the Union, and is *not* either to save or to destroy slavery. If I could save the Union without freeing *any* slave I would do it, and if I could save it by freeing *all* the slaves I would do it; and if I could save it by freeing some and leaving others alone, I would also do that. What I do about slavery and the colored race, I do because I believe it helps to save this Union; and what I forbear, I forbear because I do *not* believe it would help to save the Union. I shall do *less* whenever I shall believe what I am doing hurts the cause, and I shall do *more* whenever I shall believe doing more will help the cause. I shall try to correct errors when shown to be errors; and I shall adopt new views so fast as they shall appear to be true views.

I have here stated my purpose according to my view of *official* duty; and I intend no modification of my oft-expressed *personal* wish that all men every where could be free. Yours,

A. LINCOLN.

Lincoln's Response to Horace Greeley.
Daily National Intelligencer, Aug. 23, 1862. Library of Congress.

Filled themselves with all that is pestilent, they are, and have been, the leprous spot upon our body politic.

Enemies of our country, they deserve execration. Their mischievous and wicked acts, while benefiting neither themselves or the objects of their hypocritical sympathies, have furnished the Disunionists with the materials for their plot against the Union. It remains to be seen whether or not we are to become the victims of this plot.

...South Carolina wishes to get rid of a tariff, throw her port open, and have free trade with all the world, so as to build up a great importing city at Charleston. That may be very advantageous to South Carolina, but how is it to benefit us? Again, although all the Southern States are alike interested in the preservation and protection of the institution of slavery, yet, the interest of the cotton States, and our interest in that institution, are in one particular diametrically opposite.

Our interest in the slave is his price, theirs his labor. We estimate him by what he will bring in market, they value him for the cotton he can produce. We sell slaves, they buy them. It is to our interest that slaves shall be high, it is to their interest that they shall be cheap.

Many persons think that to carry out this favorite idea of getting negroes cheap; the cotton States would like to re-open the African slave trade, and we all know how destructive to the value of our slave property such a measure would be. But we are told now that there is nothing of it...But while I believe a majority of the southern people are opposed to renewing that traffic, I am satisfied there are many politicians in the cotton States who desire it...

South Carolina has for years been wishing herself out of the Union. A member of her Convention said, the other day, after the secession ordinance had passed, that they had now accomplished what every son of "Carolina" had been laboring for during the last thirty years. If she ever loved the Union, she has long since lost that affection.

To her the Union is the symbol of all that is hateful...We have been accustomed to regard it as a precious heritage won for us by our ancestors at the price of toil and blood...he who can entertain and deliberately express such a sentiment as that, deserves to take rank in his country's history upon the dark page which holds the names of Aaron Burr and Benedict Arnold...[34]

Shortly after Lincoln's election in November 1860, rumors circulated in North Carolina's seaboard counties that President James Buchanan planned to send a large force to occupy the local coastal fort system, including Fort Caswell and Fort Johnston near the port of Wilmington. Those bastions were located some twenty miles to the south on the Cape Fear River.[35]

Fort Caswell was located four miles south of Smithville (modern Southport) and was built in 1825. This was a large, pentagonal masonry fort intended to protect the entrance to the Cape Fear River as well as command shipping lanes in the ocean with long-range cannons.[36]

The fort had capacity for sixty-one channel bearing guns mounted *en-barbette* (on an earth mound atop the walls) and was once thought to be one of the strongest forts in the world, although it had gradually deteriorated over the years. By 1861 only two cannons were there, each mounted on rapidly decaying wooden carriages, rendering them useless for battle. Fort Johnston was much smaller and was named for colonial Provincial Governor Gabriel Johnston. Constructed in 1749, to defend the area against the French and Spanish, it was the first fort built in North Carolina. In July 1775, a group of Whigs stormed the Fort and burned most of the buildings, the first open act of defiance against King George III. In 1795, congress had it rebuilt.

Despite their strategic locations, both Fort Johnston and Fort Caswell were placed on "caretaker status" by the government several years earlier, and each had only one soldier garrisoning the fort in 1861. Their primary duties included little more than supervising the civilians who fished on the beaches in front of the fort and had little to do with anything related to real military activities in those years. With little else to do, the bored garrison soldiers regularly claimed his "cut" of the locals' catch.[37]

Even with such informality, local citizens were well-aware that controlling these forts was crucial to preventing the Port of Wilmington being sealed off by blocking the Cape Fear River. They were especially incensed by Ellis's reluctance to ally with neighboring Southern states encouraging secession, particularly South Carolina. On the day South Carolina left the Union, local militia artillery batteries fired a one hundred gun salute in the streets of Wilmington, causing no small concern among the citizens, many of whom were still strongly pro-Union.[38]

Locals in the southeastern counties of North Carolina also knew that it would be nearly impossible to retake the forts if Lincoln fully garrisoned them. A delegation from Wilmington approached Ellis immediately after he was sworn into office for his second term and asked him to approve seizure of the two forts. Ellis refused and admonished them on the basis that as long as North Carolina remained in the Union, such an act would be taken as overt hostility.[39]

The residents' fears later piqued when a newspaper from Washington, D.C., told the *Wilmington Journal* on January 8, 1861, that the U.S. ship, the *Harriett Lane*, was in-bound to help strengthen Fort Caswell and was thought to be carrying "50 men and 8 guns." Another dispatch posited on January 9, 1861, that the U.S. cutter *Forward* had left Wilmington, Delaware, armed with four cannons and forty soldiers under orders to take possession of Fort Caswell. Each report turned out to be false, but sufficiently aggravated citizens on North Carolina's coast to the degree that they expected an imminent attack on their shores.[40]

Growing political unrest combined with inaccurate news reports of an imminent Federal invasion gave locals fresh wounds, as many were still stinging from Governor Ellis' refusal to endorse capturing the two forts located below Wilmington. Whether the threat was real or not, this caused an even deeper sense of resentment along the coastal areas toward government officials, whom they perceived weren't listening to them, and were now certain would not protect them. On January 8, 1861, Mississippi became the second state to secede.[41]

A few weeks earlier, the Fort Sumter garrison commander, Major Robert Anderson, begged President Buchanan for reinforcements and supplies to bolster the fort's defenses, should the already angry and secession minded locals decide to take it by force. Buchanan, of course declined, but extant political pressure required that he take some action. Buchanan had earlier told South Carolina Governor Francis Pickens on December 16, 1860, that any attack on U.S. forts along the coast would be considered as an act of war, and that he considered secession "to be revolution."[42]

On January 12, 1861, General Winfield Scott learned that Federal sailors were arrested carrying copies of orders to reinforce Fort Pickens at Pensacola, Florida, which were taken from them. They were paroled, but Scott was furious, and ordered another steamer carrying troops to turn back. He later wrote, "Thus, those authorities have not ceased to make war upon the United States," after the Floridians captured the United States Navy yard there on January 12, 1861.[43]

President James Buchanan. Library of Congress.

Recognizing the implication of his words were a threat, Buchanan ordered a steamer bearing supplies to reinforce Fort Sumter, South Carolina, on January 4, 1861. Buchanan's attention was then also focused on dealing with the divided Congress whom he advised on January 8, 1861, that the situation was out of presidential control, and that the conflict should be allowed to go to a national vote before it turned into a full-scale war.

On January 9, 1861, Buchanan was displeased to learn of Mississippi's secession the day previous, but his correspondence from this period suggests that he was then quite distracted by a potentially dangerous situation involving U.S. Secretary of War John Floyd of Virginia, of which he was previously unaware.[44]

Since 1859, Floyd was in frequent communication with Governors of other Southern states seeking to increase their supply of Federal arms; most of which was done out of Buchanan's sight. When he finally realized Floyd's agenda, Buchanan sent an inquiry to Congress on January 9, 1861, asking whether they knew if any removal of arms or munitions from the U.S. arsenal at Harper's Ferry had occurred or not. This erupted into a scandal against Floyd, who had quietly relocated some 250,000 arms into Southern arsenals since 1859.[45]

Meanwhile, a government contract steamer, *Star of the East*, was carrying supplies and troops bound for Fort Sumter, arrived at Charleston Harbor on January 9, 1861. The ship was fired upon by cadets from the South Carolina Military Academy (later renamed the Citadel), a state-governed military academy, striking it twice, forcing the pilot to turn back. News of this incident quickly reached Wilmington, along with word that Florida and Alabama had both seceded.[46]

Coastal citizens, influenced by newspapers and rumors of a pending invasion triggered by Buchanan's promise to reinforce coastal forts, and the incident at Charleston Harbor, believed that Governor John Ellis wasn't going to protect them, and were discussing taking matters into their own hands; this was not without historic precedent, however. Eighty-six years earlier, Wilmington leaders formed a Committee of Safety in anticipation of a British invasion. On January 10, 1861, a group of prominent citizens met and formed another Committee of Safety at the New Hanover County Courthouse to discuss how best to defend the town.[47]

Hence, with the news of recent armed resistance against Buchanan's attempt to reinforce the garrison at Fort Sumter fresh in their memory, the city officials were polarized in their desire to act. After a lengthy debate, the Wilmington Committee of Safety concluded there was no way to amicably resolve their differences with the government and called for volunteers to immediately organize a home guard to deal with the crisis.[48]

It is important to grasp the context in which the speculation and rumors of the anticipated occupation emerged. While many residents of coastal North Carolina were anxious about the recent election of Abraham Lincoln, not only was he not yet in office during January 1861, but neither he nor President James Buchanan had in fact announced any concrete plans to invade their coast. Despite the latter, coastal residents' fears were heavily influenced by rumors of an imminent invasion, as their fears and unrest grew.

Although General Winfield Scott made several attempts to secure authorization from Buchanan to send some 300 troops and supplies to reinforce Fort Pickens and the Pensacola Navy Yard in late 1860, Federal steamers from Norfolk, Virginia, were not actually underway to Florida, (not North Carolina) until January 12, 1861, and the soldiers had specific orders to "commit no acts of hostility" unless the fort was attacked.[49]

According to Scott, Buchanan should have acted much earlier to protect the government's southern coastal fort system, instead of essentially stalling until he left office. The president had negotiated a sort of armistice with Southern Congressional leaders and scheduled a Peace Conference to occur in Washington, D.C., in February, which prevented the reinforcements sent earlier in January from acting more aggressively. On the other hand, Lincoln had as of yet made no statement that he intended to abolish slavery, despite his dislike of the practice, stating it was his "oft-expressed personal wish that all men everywhere could be free…"[50]

Horace Greeley, editor of the *New York Tribune,* published an editorial on August 20, 1862, entitled, "The Prayer of Twenty Million" challenging President-elect Abraham Lincoln to publicly acknowledge that slavery was the exclusive cause of the war and take immediate action for emancipation. Lincoln's response appeared in the Washington, D.C. based *Daily National Intelligencer,* a few days later.[51]

Instead, Lincoln responded by clarifying that his immediate goal was to save the Union,

IRRECONCILABLE DIFFERENCES

> My paramount object in this struggle is to save the Union, and is not either to save or destroy slavery. If I could save the Union without freeing any slave, I would do it, and if I could save it by freeing all the slaves, I would do it; and if I could save it by freeing all the slaves, I would do it; and if I could save it by freeing some and leaving others alone, I would also do that.[52]

One historian contends that even after the war began, Lincoln's intent was not to conquer the South militarily, but to suppress the insurrection economically and with the assistance of Southern unionists. Known as the Anaconda Plan, Lincoln relied upon General Winfield Scott to initiate a means of gradually shutting down the Southern economy, but isolating the cotton and other trade, hoping to achieve,

> ...a limited and relatively bloodless conflict. In May of 1861, General Winfield Scott devised a strategy of limited warfare. Instead of invading the South, he proposed to envelop it with a "complete blockade of the Atlantic and Gulf ports" and a "powerful movement down the Mississippi to the ocean, with a cordon of posts at proper points...."[53]

Yet, despite Lincoln's stated intentions, speculation and rumor led to what amounted to a general panic on North Carolina's southeastern coast, causing the Wilmington Committee of Safety to eventually take matters into their own hands. On January 12, 1861, at Washington, D.C., Lincoln's soon-to-be Secretary of State, William Seward, was trying to negotiate a peaceful settlement with Southern Congressional leaders.

Seward stated he was willing to accept the recent proposition to allow slavery to remain in existing states and territories, and enforce fugitive slave laws, which was essentially a guarantee that slavery would remain constitutional in the United States. Seward also told Southern representatives, including those from North Carolina, that more states seceding would inevitably lead to war.

Despite the seemingly conciliatory gesture, Southern representatives told Seward that any attempt to invade the Southern states would be "punished according to law." They also contended that while Seward appeared disposed to settle, his plan was not favorable toward the South. Other states, such as Virginia, were equally put off and declined

Seward's offer. One representative admonished state officials to "Let none be deceived by reports of Seward's speech yesterday. It was fraudulent and tricky under the cloak of seeming mildness with no offer of concession worth consideration."[54]

Inevitably, more states soon seceded, with Georgia leaving the Union on January 19, 1861, followed by Louisiana on January 26, 1861, and Texas on February 1, 1861. In another attempt to reconcile, a peace congress was formed at Washington on February 4, 1861, that included George Davis, a prominent attorney from Wilmington. The peace congress was intended to negotiate an honorable and amicable adjustment of the sectional differences using modifications drafted by the state of Virginia in the recent Crittenden Resolutions. The entire country was yet "convulsed with conflicting emotions." In closed sessions lasting three weeks, the representatives debated but were unable to establish a compromise that each side agreed upon when it concluded.[55]

Library of Congress.

The *Wilmington Journal* was a strongly pro-secession news organ and editorialized on February 21, 1861, that Southern states who had either seceded or planned to secede would not support the Crittenden Compromise, noting that "it is too late…" to discuss compromise, and that a peace congress would likely fail. The editor further opined "The border Southern States must decide to which Confederacy they will attach themselves… There can be no half-way course now."[56]

The U.S. Congress voted to adopt a joint resolution amending the Constitution to protect slavery where it existed on March 2, 1861. The amendment contained built in protection from future modifications by Congress, which would ostensibly protect Southern interests. Even with a visit from recently elected Abraham Lincoln and the new amendment, the peace congress was unable to resolve North-South differences.

The *Wilmington Daily Herald* reported a brief but telling anecdote on March 4, 1861, that while at the conference, Lincoln was approached by a wealthy New York shipping merchant who inquired whether he would yield to the South's "just demands", and not go to war on account of slavery. Lincoln supposedly replied, "I do not know that I understand your meaning… Nor do I know what acts or opinions may be in the future—I will defend the Constitution as it is."[57]

George Davis and the four other delegates then returned to North Carolina in frustration. Davis spoke to a large crowd at Thalian Hall in Wilmington on March 2, 1861, telling of the peace congress results, which were not favorable. The *Wilmington Daily Herald* further reported on March 4 that Davis explained that in spite of his effort to help attain a fair and honorable settlement, their differences were irreconcilable, and he would never accept the plan proposed there because he believed it to be inconsistent with the rights, interests, and dignity of the state of North Carolina.

Afterward, many leaders in North Carolina believed that secession was inevitable. Ironically, New York City had also considered secession in January 1861, so it is not surprising to hear of such a conversation with Lincoln. The mayor told the City Council there that as so many Southern states were then seceding or showing inclination to do so, that New York City should consider doing likewise and become a "free city" in order to maintain economic ties to the South, as the city was essentially dependent upon Southern cotton exports.[58]

The reader should understand that the 1850s political mindset of most civilian and military leaders was heavily influenced by the work of Constitutional Law scholar William Rawle (1759-1836). Rawle authored a textbook on constitutional law used at West Point and at most law schools of the era. He generally taught that secession was dependent upon the will of the people of a given state, and if they desire a change in government, no power in the Federal government could legally stop it.

Rawle drew the basis of his argument from Thomas Jefferson, whose beliefs are imbedded in the Declaration of Independence. Rawle believed that Jefferson wanted to clearly separate Federal authority from state powers, which he believed to be sovereign. Rawle's influence, as well as the Anti-Federalist sentiment, had taken strong in North Carolina, especially on the southeastern coast.

During the 1787—1789 debates over ratifying the Constitution, the state was divided because many residents recalled decades of Parliamentary abuses of the colonial era and were extremely skeptical of allowing the states to yield more power to what became the Federal government. These sentiments had changed little by 1861, and in this context, governing leaders of both local and state authorities in North Carolina had to face the reality that secession was imminent when the peace congress failed to bring about a mutual solution to sectional differences.[59]

Summarily, a complex combination of political and sociological factors on North Carolina's southeastern coast led to an unauthorized takeover of two United States garrisoned forts near Wilmington by local militia in January 1861. However, before examining the details of the militia's capture of Fort Caswell and Fort Johnston in January 1861, it is important to first understand the state of affairs within the militia system in North Carolina, and the political and social context in which the militia existed during the antebellum period through January 1861.

CHAPTER THREE

ANTEBELLUM MILITIA AND VOLUNTEER COMPANIES

North Carolina's state militia forces were largely ignored by state authorities following the Mexican War in 1848, although this changed in 1860 when rumors of war escalated across the state. The extant militia system was based on the Federal Militia Act of 1792, which authorized each state to keep a militia for defense purposes. All white males aged eighteen to forty-five years were required to enroll in a local company of state militia or volunteer company unless exempted by religion, occupation, or regular military service. Examples of exempt occupations included clergymen, postal employees, doctors, and the county sheriff.

North Carolina was divided into six districts by the state Adjutant General, each comprising a brigade under the command of a brigadier general. The brigade commander reported to a major general who, in turn, reported to the governor. Each county in North Carolina was further sub-divided into militia districts beginning in October 1777, and a militia captain was appointed in each district.[60]

In the period following the Revolutionary War through 1860, various militia officers attempted to reorganize the enrolled militia in each

North Carolina county on several occasions but were unable to realize any further levels of military preparedness largely due to neglect by the state authorities. Between 1781 and 1793 for example, the state militia was largely a paper tiger adorning the adjutant general's office in Raleigh. The military districts appear to have been an arrangement more for the convenience of state tax collectors than military objective, as they were concordant with those found on state tax rolls.[61]

In 1793 the state militia was reorganized into two divisions consisting of one to two brigades but still only met for drill annually, barely enough for officers to learn the names of their men, much less morph into combat-ready units. In 1822, Davidson County was added to the 7th Brigade.

Later in 1838, North Carolina then assigned numerical designations to its militia units. One district had four infantry companies of one hundred men each on paper; for example, a company would be assigned to the 63d Brigade and attached to the 4th Division. However, each division lacked a major general in command, leaving official decisions largely up to local officers.

Despite more than forty years' dormancy, the North Carolina militia was activated for a brief period in 1812 out of fear of another British invasion, and again in the 1840s following the Nat Turner Rebellion, when a group of enslaved persons in Virginia killed fifty-five people, fifty-one of whom were white.[62]

Although some local county militia units managed to maintain enough active members to hold annual muster days during this era, according to one officer, the time invested in drill was "…almost wholly thrown away – skill is not acquired – discipline is not enforced – it remains very problematical whether the training of half a century has added a single item to our stock of military skills…." The latter was largely attributed to the general "innate distaste for discipline" found among peacetime militia members.[63]

While the state militia slowly eroded into disorganized apathy, volunteer companies emerged in popularity during the 1850s, on the other hand. These private military groups were also authorized under the Federal Militia Act of 1792. Normally, they were given a great deal of latitude with regard to their uniforms, rules, and weaponry. These unique companies, many of which had existed since the late 1700s, also

ANTEBELLUM MILITIA AND VOLUNTEER COMPANIES

Generals and Field Officers, North Carolina Militia, 1813. Plate by Donald J. Long. Used with permission of the artist and the Company of Military Historians.

Fayetteville Independent Light Infantry, North Carolina Militia, 1834-1853. Plate by Donald J. Long. Used with permission of the artist and the Company of Military Historians.

TREASON ON THE CAPE FEAR

Fayetteville Light Infantry circa 1850s. Plate by Donald J. Long. Used with permission of the artist and the Company of Military Historians.

Wilmington Light Infantry Armory, circa 1892. Courtesy Cape Fear Museum.

often had their own armories. The Wilmington Light Infantry did not acquire theirs until 1892, however.

While the Militia Act of 1792 required line militia to bear arms and drill, there was little emphasis on standards for uniforms and state militia members, who normally wore civilian clothing to annual musters, if they bothered to show up at all. In contrast, volunteer companies usually demonstrated a high level of *esprit de corps*, and many sought to approximate the uniform standards of the regular army. Yet, because their garb and accoutrements were paid for by local benefactors or directly out of the officers' personal finances, they tended to be quite ornate, albeit typically gaudy and impractical, favoring styles worn during the earlier Napoleonic era.

In contrast to the careless demeanor of most state militia during antebellum, companies drilled more frequently and took pride in their military bearing. As a result, they were generally better trained and disciplined than the state militia. By the time the Civil War approached in 1860, many state authorities believed the volunteer companies would eventually replace the enrolled militia as a rapid response force in case of attack.[64]

This later proved true for dozens of volunteer companies who turned out for immediate deployment after the war erupted in 1861, while the state militia still floundered. Membership in a volunteer company was largely viewed as a status symbol of the middle-to-upper classes since the members were primarily young men from the most affluent families in the area.

The social status afforded by membership in such a company reinforced a strong sense of elitism and was looked upon with pride by the general community, in contrast to militia membership which was generally viewed as an arduous task that most men preferred to avoid altogether. As a result, young men enlisting in an antebellum volunteer company typically used their membership to catapult aspiring political careers or otherwise advance their social standing.

Typically, potential enlistees seeking membership in antebellum-era volunteer companies required a majority vote before acceptance, a practice that helped them avoid filling their ranks with less desirable members, i.e., those with more limited financial resources. Another factor evidencing their selectiveness was the high cost of uniforms and equipment. Most of the companies' uniforms were privately purchased, and the ensemble often cost upwards of ten to fifteen dollars, a goodly sum for anyone in that era.

Their weapons were privately purchased or in many cases, issued by the state. For the latter, officers were required to provide an acceptable cash bond to the governor for those arms, and they were responsible for the guns' safekeeping, as they were property of the state. Obviously, only wealthy young men could normally afford to serve in volunteer companies since those of lesser socioeconomic status generally lacked the funds to do so. The young elite of wealthy Southern towns were known for their ostentatious, presumptive demeanor in the 1850s, and usually took "...undue pride in the wealth of their parents and spurned the society of mechanics for fear their reputations would be spoiled...."[65]

However, occasionally an exception was made for those who were particularly promising, and company officers would make arrangements to cover the costs for the youth's arms, uniforms, and accoutrements. The elitism was not universal in North Carolina, however, as one of the volunteer companies emerging in the Wilmington area during the 1850s was comprised of German and Irish immigrants from working class families with little, if any, interest in climbing social ladders. Known as the German Volunteers, this outfit quickly enlisted as Company A, 8th North Carolina Volunteers, in 1861.[66]

German Volunteers at the old Courthouse, Wilmington, North Carolina, circa 1859.
Courtesy Lower Cape Fear Historical Society.

2nd Lt. Hanke Vollers, German Volunteers, circa 1860. Courtesy Volley Hanson.

As earlier noted, volunteer companies tended to have a strong *esprit de corps*, as evidenced by their well-organized musters and frequent drills and high discipline level. They drilled more frequently and intensively than their counterparts in the enrolled county or state militia, who generally viewed drill as a nuisance.

During antebellum, militia muster days were usually a center of the local activity because of the number of influential people involved, but several period sources also reveal that militia muster days tended to be very unruly, with drunken brawls in lieu of discipline and drill. This was in great contrast to the fanfare and officious tone of volunteer company muster days, which were usually accompanied by martial music provided by local brass bands.

One such company was the Wilmington Light Infantry, who regularly participated in formal ceremonies and parades during the 1850s. This company organized on May 20, 1853, with Mexican War veteran Edward P. Chrysostom Cantwell elected as first captain. Cantwell graduated from Harvard University with a law degree at age twenty-one-years, and in 1847 was commissioned as 2nd Lieutenant of Company G, Twelfth Infantry Regiment in the regular army, and served in the Mexican War.[67]

Edward P. Chrysostom Cantwell. Courtesy Cape Fear Museum.

That regiment was comprised of North Carolinians, and while serving in Mexico, young Lieutenant Cantwell fought in several major battles including National Bridge, where he was the "first to wave" the national colors over the fort. He was also engaged at Cerro Gordo, Las Animas, Jalapa, Huamantala, and Atlixco, and was in numerous other smaller skirmishes.[68]

His commander, Captain Charles R. Jones of Iredell County, North Carolina, was granted permission to retain the national flag, consisting of twenty-eight stars and thirteen stripes as well as nine bullet holes, by Major General Winfield S. Scott when the 12th Regiment reached Mexico City. On February 22, 1857, Jones, then a brigadier general of militia, presented the flag to the Wilmington Light Infantry; Edward Cantwell requested the flag be returned to him, and in 1859, the Wilmington Light Infantry by unanimous resolution presented the banner "to the keeping of him [Cantwell] who first raised it victoriously in defense of his country."[69]

When the Civil War began, Cantwell was concerned the flag would be destroyed, and buried it on an island in the Cape Fear River. The flag remained there until 1863, when Federal soldiers came to Wilmington. One day, a squad of soldiers discovered the flag and presented it to the Wilmington Fire company, who later returned it to Cantwell.[70]

His younger brother, John L. Cantwell, is said to have taken the flag staff and attached the colors of the 51st North Carolina Troops (hereafter NCT), when he was elected colonel in 1862. That flag and staff were captured in Virginia, and eventually found among the Confederate flags held by the United States War Department in June 1887.[71]

Volunteer companies generally became mainstays at political gatherings across the state during antebellum, such as visits from the governor or other heads of state served at formal events. For example, in 1857, the Fayetteville Independent Light Infantry, the second oldest independent volunteer militia company in the United States, provided an escort and honor guard for Marquis de Lafayette when he traveled to his namesake city in 1820.

While guiding Lafayette at night, the company used lighted candles in the muzzles of their muskets to light the way. The Fayetteville Light Infantry later fought with the 1st North Carolina Volunteers at the Battle of Big Bethel, Virginia on June 10, 1861.[72]

Summarily, with the state militia system in a state of disarray, the volunteer companies quickly stepped up to provide at least a facsimile of military readiness during the antebellum era, although their membership was usually limited to only those who could afford to participate.

There are exceptions to every rule, however, and in the Wilmington area there is evidence that by 1860, the state militia began drilling with volunteer outfits in hopes of increasing readiness as rumors of war circulated following Lincoln's election. This core group of local volunteers and militia soon triggered a series of events in 1861 that would forever change the course of North Carolina.

Unidentified militia member from Newbern, Craven County, North Carolina, circa 1850s. Courtesy Fred Taylor.

Unidentified North Carolina Militia Officer, likely a member of the Gaston Blues, Gaston County, North Carolina, circa 1850s. Courtesy Fred Taylor.

Lt. William Penn Metts, Newbern Light Infantry, circa 1860. Courtesy Fred Taylor.

Caption: 2nd Lt. Charles B. Cook, Fayetteville Light Infantry, circa 1860. Courtesy North Carolina State Archives.

The Duplin Rifles became Co. A, 43rd NCT in 1859.
Courtesy University of North Carolina Library.

CHAPTER FOUR

CAPTURE OF FORT CASWELL AND FORT JOHNSTON

In January 1861, Colonel John Lucas Paul Cantwell of Wilmington commanded the 30th Regiment North Carolina Militia, which was then part of the 3d Brigade, 6th Division, North Carolina Militia under Brigadier General John Cowan. Cantwell was born in 1828 at Charleston, South Carolina, the son of an Irish immigrant.[73]

He served in Palmetto Regiment, South Carolina Volunteers during the Mexican War, and relocated to Wilmington, North Carolina in the 1850s. He enlisted in the 30th North Carolina Militia and eventually became colonel. Cantwell later became Colonel of the 51st NCT and resigned in October 1862 to become Captain of Company F, 3rd NCT.[74]

Cantwell was captured at Spotsylvania in 1864 and taken to Charleston, South Carolina, where he became part of a group of prisoners of war known as the Immortal Six Hundred. This group was so named when the U.S. Secretary of War, Edwin M. Stanton, ordered that six hundred prisoners, all officers, were to be positioned on Morris Island in Charleston Harbor within direct line of fire from Confederate batteries at Fort Sumter. Stanton's order was in response to Confederate authorities similarly using a group of imprisoned and high-ranking

Union officers, including several generals, as human shields in the city of Charleston, in an attempt to prevent further Federal bombardment, which had destroyed sections of the city. Although General Ulysses S. Grant opposed prisoner exchange after 1863, President Lincoln eventually intervened and the 600 Confederate officers were transferred to Fort Pulaski, near Savannah, Georgia.[75]

Colonel John L. P. Cantwell. Private Collection.

CAPTURE OF FORT CASWELL AND FORT JOHNSTON

After the Civil War, Cantwell became a produce broker in Wilmington and kept up his connection with the Wilmington Light Infantry and with Confederate veterans' organizations. He later again served the United States during the Spanish-American War, when the 30th Regiment was something of an anomaly in comparison to other militia, as it was then thought to be the only organized regiment in the state.[76]

On January 10, 1861, the Wilmington city leaders organized a Committee of Safety and appointed a former militia captain, John J. Hedrick, as Major and placed the volunteers under his immediate command.[77]

This new ensemble deemed itself as the "Cape Fear Minutemen" and viewed their membership as "a band of patriots." Although they were armed with only shotguns and old muskets, the militiamen had enough provisions to last one week when they boarded a small schooner at the Market Street dock in Wilmington. They departed early that morning, and traveled to Smithville, (modern day Southport) arriving later that afternoon. The battalion then hastily formed up and rapidly marched to the United States barracks at Fort Johnston.[78]

U.S. Ordnance Sergeant James S. Reilly was the only soldier garrisoning Fort Johnston when they arrived there around 3:00 p.m. Startled, he found the militia standing at the front causeway demanding surrender, but he was not quick to comply. Riley reported,

> They came to my door...and demanded the keys of the magazine of me. I told them I would not give up the keys to any person with my life. They replied it was no use to be obstinate, for they had the magazine already in their possession...I considered a while and seen it was no use to persevere, for they were determined to have what ordnance stores there was at the post. I then told them if they would sign receipts for me for the ordnance...I would give it up to them....[79]

Later that afternoon, Major Hedrick also met the "The Smithville Guards" under Captain Stephen D. Thurston, a militia outfit formed at Smithville, and together with another group of roughly twenty-five men from Smithville who were "acting as civilians only," they crossed the bay some three miles to Fort Caswell. There they confronted the lone guard, U.S. Ordnance Sergeant Frederick Darlingkiller, and demanded he surrender the fort, which he did only after exchanging some words. Although unharmed, neither of the sergeants were allowed to communicate with their chain of command.[80]

Fort Caswell Causeway where the Cape Fear Minutemen confronted Sgt. Frederick Darlingkiller on January 10, 1861. Photo by author.

The Minutemen immediately began to strengthen their new position by improving the earthen works on top of the barbette. They spent two cold nights standing guard along the parapets and patrolling the beaches, but there is no evidence a shot was ever fired. Colonel Cantwell later recalled their misadventure as treason, although afterward neither the state nor Federal authorities bothered to pursue any legal recourse against them,

> Major Hedrick assumed command and prepared to make his position as secure as was possible. About twenty-five strong, armed with only shotguns, but sure of ample reinforcements should occasion arise, these brave men determined to hold Fort Caswell at all hazards.

CAPTURE OF FORT CASWELL AND FORT JOHNSTON

In bitter cold weather they stood guard on the ramparts, and patrolled the beaches, reckoning not that, unsustained even by State authority, their action was treasonable rebellion jeopardizing their lives and property. There were only two 32 pounder guns mounted, one on the sea face and one on the inner face, both carriages being too decayed to withstand their own recoil, but such as they were, with them they determined to defy the army and navy of the United States.[81]

Colonel John Jackson Hedrick.
Courtesy Lower Cape Fear Historical Society.

While holding Fort Caswell, the Minutemen had one incident causing no small alarm. Colonel Cantwell also recorded,

> The smoke of an approaching steamer being once described below the horizon the alarm was signaled, and, believing it to be a man-of-war, the brave men of Smithville flew to arms, and soon the bay was alive with boats hurrying them to the aid of their comrades within the fort. Women, as in the old days, armed sons and fathers, and urged them to the front. But the steamer proved to be friendly....[82]

At face value, Ellis was faced with a dilemma. He could either appease the irate citizens of the region or seek to maintain amicable ties to the United States. On January 11, 1861, Ellis wrote that he was deeply distressed by the affair, but he simultaneously believed their actions were,

> ...actuated by patriotic motives," mentioning nothing of treason...in view of the relations existing between the general government and the state of North Carolina, there is no authority of law, under existing circumstances, for the occupation of the United States forts situated in this state...[I] am compelled by an imperative sense of duty to order that Fort Caswell be restored to the possession of the United States.[83]

With that said, Ellis ordered Colonel Cantwell to proceed to Smithville and communicate orders to Captain Thurston to withdraw his troops from Fort Caswell. Cantwell received the orders and went to Fort Caswell where Major Hedrick was located accompanied by Major Robert E. Calder, Acting Adjutant, and Captain William Calder, Acting Quartermaster of the 30th Regiment, North Carolina Militia, on January 11, 1861. Ellis wrote,

> Sir: I have been informed, unofficially, that captain S. D. Thurston, of the Smithville Guards, has, with his company, taken possession of fort Caswell add now holds the same. My informant assured me at the same time that Capt. Thurston is a gallant officer, and was actuated by patriotic motives, as a citizen of North Carolina, in the movement referred to.

CAPTURE OF FORT CASWELL AND FORT JOHNSTON

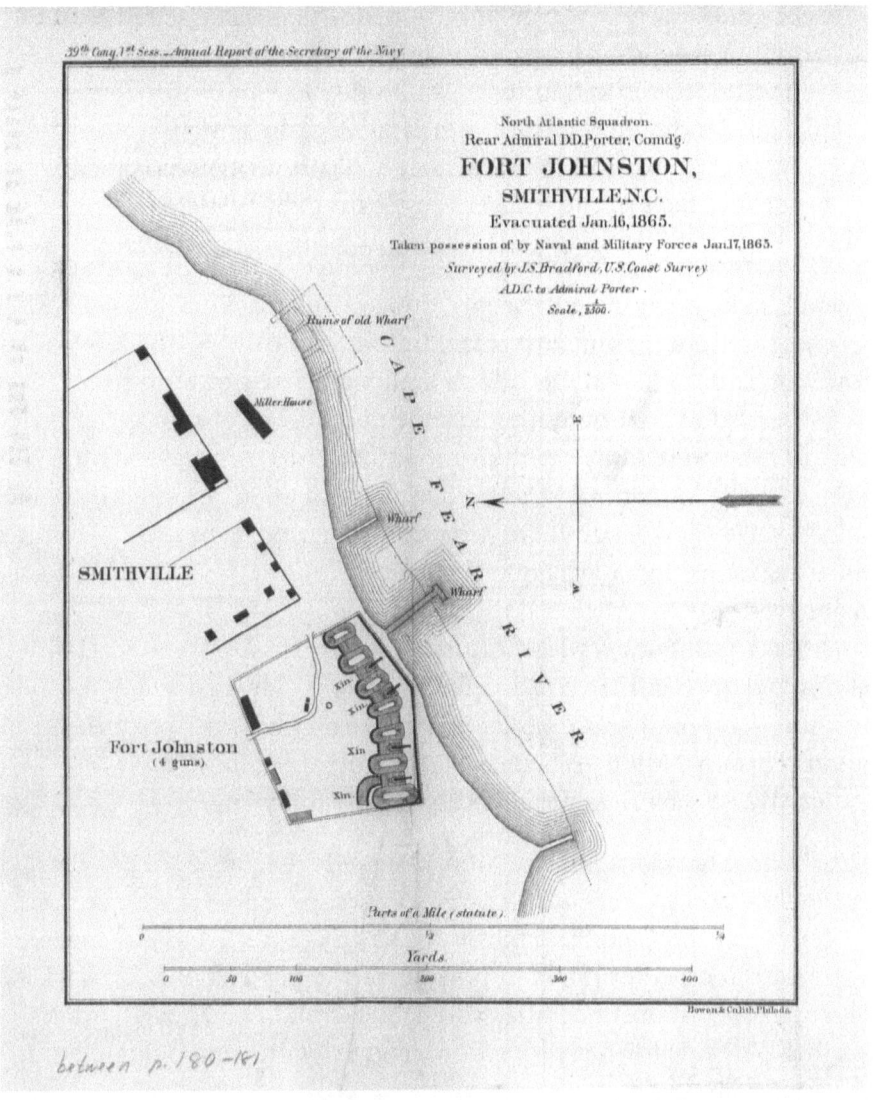

Library of Congress.

This, I doubt not, is true; yet in view of the relations existing between the general government and the State of North-Carolina, there is no authority in law, under existing circumstances, for the occupation of United States forts situated in this State.

I cannot, therefore, sustain that action of Captain Thurston, however patriotic his motives may have been, and am compelled, by an imperative sense of duty, to order that fort Caswell be restored to the possession of the authorities of the United States. You will proceed to Smithville, upon the receipt of this communication and communicate orders to Captain Thurston to withdraw his troops from fort Caswell. You will also investigate and report the facts of the transaction to this department.[84]

Upon receipt, Cantwell's entourage came to Smithville and acquired a small sailing sloop and began the journey to Fort Caswell. They became stranded about four miles below Smithville in shallow waters, however, and had to wade ashore and walk back to Smithville. They met several delays in obtaining another boat from obstinate Smithville citizens, who were aware of their intentions to return possession of the forts to Federal control. Cantwell finally attained another boat and sailed over to Fort Caswell, arriving there after dark, only to encounter more resistance from armed sentries who would not allow them to see Major Hedrick.

After arguing for a while, Cantwell's party finally accessed Hedrick, who asked to consider the matter overnight. He conceded the next morning, responding, "...we as North Carolinians will obey the command. This post will be evacuated tomorrow at 9 a.m."[85]

The Wilmington Daily Herald reported the following,

> Whereas from information deemed reliable sources that Federal troops were on the way to garrison Fort Caswell at the mouth of the Cape Fear River, which was regarded as a menace to our people and State, a portion of the citizens of Brunswick and New Hanover Counties, took possession of said Fort in order that the State for her protection, might obtain peaceable possession of the same.
>
> Therefore, Be it—Resolved, first, That we highly approve of the patriotic spirit and pure motives which prompted our fellow citizens of the above counties in their action, and that a Committee of Three be appointed to make arrangements for presenting them with some tangible evidence of our regard.
>
> Resolved, second, that in the prompt evacuation of said Fort by order of the Governor of North Carolina, they have proved themselves to be good and loyal citizens of the Old North State.

Resolved, three, That the dilatory action of our Legislature in calling a Convention may, in view of the imminent danger now threatening us and our sister Southern States, force the State into revolution, and this can only be secured by the speedy action of the Legislature in trusting this great question with the people, by doing which and by placing the State in a proper condition for defense, they may make secession peaceable.[86]

Ellis wired his apology to President Buchanan on January 12, 1861, attempting to explain the militia's actions and maintain a peaceful relationship with the United States,

> Sir: Reliable information has reached this department. that, on the 8th inst., Forts Johnston and Caswell were taken possession of by State Troops and persons resident in that vicinity, in an irregular manner. Upon receipt of this information, I immediately issued a military order requiring the forts to be restored to the authorities of the United States, which order will be executed this day.
>
> My information satisfies me that this popular outbreak was caused by a report, very generally credited, but which, for the sake of humanity, I hope it is not true, that it was the purpose of the administration to coerce the Southern States, and that troops were on their way to garrison the Southern ports and to begin the work of subjugation.
>
> This impression is not yet erased from the public mind, which is deeply agitated at the bare contemplation of so great an indignity and wrong, and I would most earnestly appeal to your Excellency to strengthen my hands in my efforts to preserve the public order here, by placing it in my power to give public assurances that no measures of force are contemplated towards us.
>
> Your Excellency will pardon me therefore for asking whether the United States forts will be garrisoned with United States troops during your administration. This question I ask in perfect respect, and with an earnest desire to prevent consequences which I know would be regretted by your Excellency as much as myself.

Should I receive assurance that no troops will be sent to this State prior to the 4th of March next, then all will be peace and quiet here, and the property of the United States will be fully protected as heretofore.

Library of Congress.

If, however, I am unable to get such assurances I will not undertake to answer for the consequences. The forts in this State have long been unoccupied and their being garrisoned at this time will unquestionably be looked upon as a hostile demonstration, and will, in my opinion, certainly be resisted.

Believing your Excellency to be sincerely desirous of preserving peace and preventing the effusion of the blood of your countrymen, I have deemed it my duty to yourself as well as to the people of North Carolina to make the foregoing enquiry and to acquaint you with the state of the public mind here.[87]

President James Buchanan replied via John Holt, U.S. Secretary of War, on January 15, 1861, applauding Ellis for taking quick action but made it clear that he would make no promise of restraint should "any future takeover or similar hostile action" occur,

Sir: Your letter of the 12th instant addressed to the President of the United States, has by him been referred to this department, and he instructs me to express his gratification at the promptitude with which you have ordered the expulsion of the lawless men who recently occupied forts Johnston and Caswell.

He regards this action on the part of your excellency, as in complete harmony with the honor and patriotic character of the people of North Carolina, whom you so worthily represent. In reply to your enquiry, whether it is the purpose of the President to garrison the forts of North-Carolina during his administration, I am directed to say that they, in common with the other forts, arsenals, and public property of the United States, are in the charge of the President, and that if assailed, no matter from what quarter or under what pretext, it is his duty to protect them by all the means which the law has placed at his disposal.

It is not his purpose to garrison the forts to which you refer at present, because he considers them entirely safe, as heretofore, under the shelter of that law-abiding sentiment for which the people of North-Carolina have ever been distinguished. Should they, however, be attacked or menaced with danger of being seized and taken from the possession of the United States, he could not escape from his constitutional obligation to defend and preserve them. The very satisfactory and patriotic assurances given by your excellency, justify him, however, in entertaining the confident expectation that no such contingency will arise.[88]

One historian later concluded this was little more than a veiled threat, as Buchanan essentially told Ellis that should North Carolina secede, that would be sufficient grounds to justify invasion of the coastal region.[89]

On January 17, 1861, the *Wilmington Journal* contained an article indicating that the *Baltimore Sun* news organ had recently and erroneously claimed that Fort Caswell and Fort Johnston were occupied by some 800 North Carolina State Troops, but the editor asserted,

> *The Sun* is mistaken about those forts…Fort Caswell has not been occupied by State Troops, but by citizens, mainly of Brunswick County. That a large sympathy with these citizens exists throughout the state is certain, and it is also certain that even among those who may have thought the movement premature, there is a determination to sustain them if necessary. Gov. Ellis cannot, as governor of the State, while in the Union, officially recognize the occupation of these forts, which is in truth under any view of the case so far, only a trespass, the talk about treason and all that to the contrary notwithstanding.[90]

Apparently, no one noticed that the inaccurate news reports and political posturing had influenced the Committee of Safety's decision, as the entire affair was largely triggered by ungrounded rumors. The two steamers presumably headed to the North Carolina coast from Washington were headed to South Carolina, where they attempted to reinforce Fort Sumter. While Governor Ellis publicly denounced the incident, what he did after the surrender of the forts is most telling. Although their actions amounted to treason under extant laws, the Cape Fear Minutemen, Smithville Guards and other 30th North Carolina Militia members involved received little more than a scolding from the governor. To the contrary, most of their officers soon received commissions in the Confederate army. This included Colonel Cantwell, who went on to command both the 51st NCT and 59th NCT.[91]

CAPTURE OF FORT CASWELL AND FORT JOHNSTON

When rumors of the Wilmington militia planning to capture the forts reached Raleigh, the House of Commons devised a series of resolutions for the governor, one specifically stating their expectations in regard to the coastal forts,

> Resolved, That his excellency, the Governor, you are requested to inform this House whether he has had any correspondence with the President of the United States, or any other officer of the State or Federal Government, relative to the occupation of Forts Caswell and Macon, or either of them, by the militia of this State, or any body of armed citizens; or as to any intention of that government to place troops in said forts; and if so, to communicate such correspondence to the House of Commons.[92]

Governor Ellis responded *ex post facto*, a few days later,

> Gentlemen: In compliance with the annexed resolution, I herewith transmit a copy of a correspondence between this department and the general government at Washington, relative to the occupation of Forts Caswell and Johnston by citizens of North Carolina.
>
> No mention was made in the correspondence of Fort Macon, for the reason that I had not heard that that fort had been in any way interfered with by our citizens. For the better understanding of the subject and the grounds of my correspondence with the general government, I herewith transmit a copy of an order issued from this department to Col. John L. Cantwell, of the 30th regiment N. C. - militia, and his report as to the manner of executing the same.
>
> This is the first opportunity I have had of laying this correspondence before your honorable body, as the letter from the Secretary of War was received by last night's mail, and the report of Col. Cantwell this morning.[93]

Governor Ellis afterward decided that despite his desire to remain in the Union, secession was likely going to occur. On January 29th, 1861, at his behest, the Assembly passed a bill authorizing a convention on the subject; just days earlier delegates were sent to a Peace Conference in Washington, which Ellis believed had little chance of success, given the hostile state of affairs.

On January 30, 1861, members of the Southern Convention were meeting at Montgomery, Alabama, with delegates from North Carolina present.[94]

Revealing his belief that secession was inevitable, Ellis advised the delegates not to wait before voting to establish a Southern government, advising, "Virginia, North Carolina, and other border slave states will much sooner join an organized government than secede without such government." Despite this, the majority of North Carolinians did not agree, as on February 28, 1861, the citizens voted to defeat his call for a secession convention.[95]

The summary lesson from events on January 10, 1861, is to consider how a state of public hysteria was generated by inaccurate newspaper accounts and rumors. One coastal resident quipped that the rumors caused, "…much chafing among her people in the eastern counties…." Regardless of whether one believes that their fears were justified or not, the actions of the coastal militia directly contributed to escalating political tensions leading to war, nearly three months before Lincoln took office. Such was the consequence of acting on fear and rumors; a majority of citizens who were previously Union supporters, now adamantly desired secession as April approached. North Carolina's citizen soldiers had drawn the sword.[96]

CHAPTER FIVE

A SERIES OF IRONIC EVENTS

Just five days after the coastal militia captured Fort Johnston and Fort Caswell, on January 15, 1861, the Fayetteville Armory received 15,480 U.S. M1842 .69 caliber smoothbore muskets by order of U.S. Secretary of War John B. Floyd. In addition, Floyd also sent 9,520 altered-to-percussion muskets and 2,000 .54 caliber Mississippi rifles from the U.S. arsenals at Springfield, Massachusetts, and Watervliet, New York, to Fayetteville, couched under the rubric of improving the Southern coastal defenses in case of foreign attack. Governor Ellis had been communicating with Floyd on this issue since June 1859, ostensibly seeking to exchange the state's antiquated supply of flintlock arms for newer ones.[97]

Floyd, a former governor of Virginia from 1849 to 1852, was outspoken and pompous, openly admonishing Southern leaders to seek peaceful redress with the government in lieu of a civil war during the 1850s. Despite this, Floyd also had a reputation for poor record keeping and was the subject of several claims of fraud and mismanagement during his political tenure. Earlier in 1859, Floyd had sold 31,600 of the old flintlock muskets to Southern arsenals at $2.60 apiece.[98]

At that time, the U.S. Army was in process of transitioning from using outdated firearms, i.e., the older flintlock smoothbore muskets, to those with the newer, more accurate percussion ignition system with a rifled barrel. As Secretary of War, Floyd was responsible for replacing the older weapons and making room in the Federal arsenals for the new ones. According to the Militia Act of 1792, each state was entitled to a quota of firearms for the militia, which was still true during antebellum. In this sense, his actions were nothing unusual by selling outdated weapons to Southern arsenals.[99]

However, by the spring of 1860, Floyd had 250,000 arms on hand in the Federal arsenals at Watervliet, New York, and Springfield, Massachusetts and at Pittsburgh, Pennsylvania. He shipped 40,000 new M1842 .69 caliber rifled percussion muskets to Southern arsenals, along with 65,000 flintlocks and another 10,000 flintlocks altered to percussion. Then, on December 20, 1860, Floyd covertly shipped 113 heavy Columbiad cannon and eleven 32 pounders from the Pittsburgh Arsenal to the federal forts at Ship Island, Mississippi, and Galveston, Texas.[100]

Both were unfinished, ungarrisoned, and completely unready for such armaments. Placing large coastal cannon in those locations later ensured quite the prize when captured by secessionists. At first glance, the transfer of muskets to Southern arsenals doesn't seem unusual given the need to make room for newer weapons; however, at the time Floyd ordered each of these transactions, neither President Buchanan nor his cabinet were aware of it. Given his reputation for questionable behavior with regard to record keeping and finances, this later led many to accuse him of treason and conspiracy, a question which is still debated today.[101]

Ellis' desire to increase the states arms supply is clearly stated in his letters to President Buchanan; however, the unusually large quantity (27,000 arms) sent to Fayetteville was not mentioned in his correspondence with the president, who knew nothing about the cache. On the other hand, there is no evidence Ellis was surprised to receive so many muskets, or that Floyd sent the weapons by mistake. At the time the arms were received, North Carolina had less than 1,500 state militia registered, a figure which increased to only around 3,000 by June 1861.[102]

Of particular interest is not simply the fact that the capture of Fort Johnston and Fort Caswell and the arms delivery from Floyd each occurred in January 1861, but that these incidents were two months prior to Lincoln's inauguration. Yet, despite the obvious irony, there is no hard evidence proving that Ellis was conspiring with Floyd to secede at that point.

Floyd, however, became the focus of a major financial scandal in December 1860, involving mismanagement of Indian Bonds. This added to the outrage from Pittsburgh citizens who recently learned that he had shipped several pieces of coastal artillery southward from the Pittsburgh Arsenal. When South Carolina seceded, Buchanan was forced to demand Floyd's resignation.

John B. Floyd. Library of Congress.

Floyd resisted, although ultimately resigned from office on December 29, 1860. He was still quite powerful, and using his contacts, later acquired a commission as a brigadier general in 1861. He proved to be an inept commander, however, and was shamed by the newspapers after surrendering to General Ulysses S. Grant during the Fort Donelson campaign in February 1862.[103]

North Carolina wasted no time putting Floyd's generous gift to use, however, and quickly issued the entire stash of new weapons at the Fayetteville arsenal to volunteer regiments shortly after the state's secession in April 1861. Obviously, one of the byproducts of John Floyd's covert arms delivery was that the militia and volunteer companies accepted the reality of impending civil war.

United States Arsenal at Fayetteville, March 1865.
Courtesy University of North Carolina Library.

Once they received word that 27,000 new weapons were stashed at the Fayetteville Arsenal, officers from both volunteer and state militia companies across the state hastily inventoried their units' outdated firearms and equipment, and immediately began soliciting the state Adjutant General to acquire the newer weapons.

The *Carolina Watchman* in Salisbury, North Carolina, earlier reported a mass meeting of Union men there on January 29, 1861. The gathering was held at the request of the state legislature to consider secession and discuss increasing preparations for war, including increasing both the frequency and intensity of training for the state militia. Delegates were nominated to inform state lawmakers of local sentiments. Several officers of local militia, the Rowan Rifle Guards and Rowan Artillery were present at this meeting.[104]

Following the recent capture of coastal forts, a sense of imminent danger rapidly spread throughout the state. The state militia were keenly aware that the tense political scenario could have serious consequences on their lives, and especially the volunteers, who now recognized that unit membership was no longer merely a tool for acquiring social status.

March 1861 was therefore a time of intense political changes and apprehension in North Carolina. On March 5, 1861, the results of the state secession meetings were announced, and it was clear that in some counties, including Rowan County where Governor Ellis was from, the "Union sentiment" still prevailed.[105]

A significant part of the state population was beginning to oppose remaining in the Union, however, as John Brunner, the editor of the *Carolina Watchman*, offered a brief description of one of the strange new flags secessionist minded citizens had posted at a local hotel on March 5, 1861:

> Disunionists disgruntled over defeat hoist disunion flag over Mansion Motel. This strange bunting consists in the center of a cross, seven well defined and seven or eight outlined stars filling the four prongs of the cross. It has little beauty to attract, and we trust will never become the standard of those who have lived so prosperously and happily beneath the protection of the stars and stripes under which our liberty was gained by the fathers of the Revolution.[106]

In spite of rapidly spreading secession ardor, Brunner further admonished citizens to "stand firm and work like patriots" to keep North Carolina in the Union; the same editor also later opined on March 19, 1861, that "future historians will award highest praises to those who held out the longest...." In neighboring South Carolina, some citizens perceived that North Carolina was indeed dragging its heels in secession due to strong unionist sentiments; one woman wrote in her diary, "N.C. seems in no hurry to join us, she certainly can't be called hasty."[107]

With a newfound sense of urgency, the state militia began drilling more frequently during this apprehensive period. Yet, despite an ominous political forecast, volunteer units around the state continued to make regular appearances at various ceremonies. For example, a gala military ceremony was held at Greensboro on March 25, 1861, that included three well-known volunteer outfits, the Orange Guards, Rowan Rifle Guards, and the Guilford Grays.[108]

Those outfits drilled together and paraded that day commemorating the eighty-fifth anniversary of the Revolutionary War battle at Guilford Courthouse. The gala ceremony was hosted by the Guilford Grays, who formed in 1855, and later became Company B, 27th NCST. The Orange Grays became Company G, 27th NCST while the Rowan Rifles later became Company K, 4th NCST during the summer of 1861. The sight of such companies drilling together was construed by one observer as a show of military force in favor of secession. This was likely because each of these companies hailed from strongly pro-Union or "No Convention" counties.[109]

On the other hand, as another testimony to the self-serving side of human nature, even during those last days of peacetime, the winds of war were blowing fast across the North Carolina countryside. Suddenly, many opportunistic militia officers resigned, and sought commissions in newly forming regiments they thought more likely to see action across the state.[110]

One of President Lincoln's first actions after calling for 75,000 volunteers was also requesting additional troops to hold coastal forts in Georgia, Alabama, Mississippi, Louisiana, and Florida. The *Fayetteville Observer*, a strongly Union newspaper, reported on April 4, 1861,

> The President has made a requisition on all the Confederate states for 5,000 additional troops for service at Fort Pickens. The contingents are as follows: Alabama 1500 men; Georgia 1000; Mississippi 1000; Louisiana 1000 and Florida 500. No requisition has been made up on South Carolina, because your state has so large a force in the field before Fort Sumter.

A SERIES OF IRONIC EVENTS

The War Department is vigorously concentrating men and materials at various important points and preparing an extensive scale for defensive operations. Competent officers and agents have been despatched to the Indian frontier, and means will be amply and judiciously used to quiet the disturbances. Advice received by the State Department from Washington give the most positive assurances that Fort Pickens will ultimately be given up.[111]

Thus, while many North Carolinians adamantly wanted to remain in the Union, the majority were now leaning toward secession. Governor Ellis, a realist, likewise recognized secession was inevitable, although would not yet occur.

CHAPTER SIX

COASTAL FORTS RETAKEN

In response to the attack on Fort Sumter of April 12, 1861, and its surrender one day later, President Abraham Lincoln issued a call for 75,000 volunteers on April 17, 1861. He then dispatched the U.S. Secretary of War, Simon Cameron, to inform Governor John Ellis that he wanted North Carolina to provide two regiments to help suppress the rebellion. Lincoln's request offended all of Ellis' sensibilities; at first, he did not believe the request was from Lincoln himself, but he flatly responded with a telegram to Simon Cameron, on April 15, 1861, stating:

> Your dispatch is received, and if genuine, which its extraordinary character leads me to doubt, I have to say in reply, that I regard the levy of troops made by the administration for the purpose of subjugating the states of the South, as a violation of the Constitution, and as a gross usurpation of power.
>
> I can be no party to this wicked violation of the laws of the country and to this war upon the liberties of a free people. You can get no troops from North Carolina....

Other Southern states were already pushing for immediate secession, and this event locked the wheels in motion for North Carolina's withdrawal from the Union on May 20, 1861. When Lincoln's demand

Bombardment of Fort Sumter. Library of Congress.

Interior of Fort Sumter following the attack. Library of Congress.

was announced, the local volunteer companies "made the event the subject of rejoicing by firing cannon" in Salisbury, North Carolina.[112]

In an ironic twist of circumstance, Ellis wasted no time retaking the coastal forts on April 15, defying the previous warning from former President James Buchanan. On April 14, he sent orders to Colonel John Cantwell stating, "to take Forts Caswell and Johnston without delay and hold them until further orders against all comers."[113]

Colonel Cantwell immediately mustered his 30th North Carolina Militia that day, with orders to "the officers in command of the Wilmington Light Infantry, the German Volunteers, and the Wilmington Rifle Guards, and the Cape Fear Light Artillery (formerly the Cape Fear Minutemen) to assemble fully armed and equipped this afternoon" which was promptly obeyed.[114]

The 30th North Carolina Militia mustered along with another 120 men from four volunteer companies, the Wilmington Light Infantry under Captain W.L. DeRossett; the German Volunteers under Captain C. Cornehlson; the Wilmington Rifle Guards under Captain John Meares (recall that earlier in March 1861 Meares led a public meeting at Whitesville, North Carolina, arguing to stay in the Union) and the Cape Fear Light Artillery under Lieutenant James M. Stevenson. Note that Major John J. Hedrick was in command of the artillery but was then away on official business in Raleigh seeking supplies for the militia.

The German Volunteers and the Wilmington Light Infantry were each formed in 1853. Along with the Wilmington Rifle Guards, these companies mustered into the 8th North Carolina Volunteers in 1861, and were later designated as Companies A, G, and I, respectively, of the 18th NCT. That regiment carried a heavy burden after the May 2, 1863, Battle of Chancellorsville; many scholars believe soldiers in this regiment fired the musket volley that mortally wounded General Thomas "Stonewall" Jackson.

The Cape Fear Artillery was organized by Major John Hedrick and became Battery C, 36th NCST. Adding to the irony, Fort Johnston was similarly captured from the British by angry citizens in 1775, and in 1766, coastal residents gave the armed resistance to the British Stamp Act by refusing to allow the Kings Tax Officials to disembark boats at the nearby Brunswick settlement, only some 30 miles north of Smithville. With his forces thus mustered, Cantwell directed his troops to the docks on Market Street and again hastily boarded two steamers bound for Smithville.[115]

Ellis again contacted Colonel Cantwell early on the morning of April 16, admonishing his militia to proceed at once to the forts and "take possession of the same in the name of the State of North Carolina. This measure being one of precaution only, you will observe strictly a peaceful policy and act only on defensive."

Upon reaching the dock at Smithville, the militia marched roughly a half-mile to Fort Johnston, where they found the fort still garrisoned of only one man, the hapless career army ordnance sergeant James Reilly, who by now was a case study in classic military ironies. Reilly was the same soldier garrisoning the fort when the Cape Fear Minutemen captured it in January 1861, and once again had to face an armed mob of angry citizens alone.

Much to his chagrin, Reilly listened once more as the militia demanded the surrender of his garrison around 4:00 p.m. when they arrived at Fort Johnston. This time he was quite argumentative, but he eventually begrudgingly surrendered.[116]

Meanwhile, the Cape Fear Artillery were detailed to hold the fort, while the rest of the militia departed for Fort Caswell. They arrived there in late afternoon and once more found Sgt. Frederick Darlingkiller and two other men. One man identified only as "Sgt. Walker," made several attempts to contact his officers. His actions resulted in his close confinement, but no one was harmed. Once again, the mason forts guarding the entrance to the Cape Fear River were in the hands of North Carolina militia.[117]

After hearing the news about Lincoln's demand for troops, Ellis immediately alerted the state militia and volunteer companies around the state. Four days later, some 1,000 men of the 4th Brigade of North Carolina Militia, comprised of the 33d Regiment North Carolina Militia and the Fayetteville Light Infantry, captured the Federal Arsenal at Fayetteville with over 30,000 muskets and other ordnance, including the recently acquired 27,000 arms from former U.S. Secretary of War, John Floyd.

Once the news of the captures reached the press, several established volunteer companies tendered their service to Ellis, who quickly

BY THE PRESIDENT OF THE UNITED STATES.
A PROCLAMATION.

Whereas the laws of the United States have been, for some time past, and now are, opposed, and the execution thereof obstructed, in the States of South Carolina, Georgia, Alabama, Florida, Mississippi, Louisiana, and Texas, by combinations too powerful to be suppressed by the ordinary course of judicial proceedings, or by the powers vested in the Marshals by law :

Now, therefore, I, Abraham Lincoln, President of the United States, in virtue of the power in me vested by the Constitution and the laws, have thought fit to call forth, and hereby do call forth, the militia of the several States of the Union, to the aggregate number of seventy-five thousand, in order to suppress said combinations, and to cause the laws to be duly executed.

The details for this object will be immediately communicated to the State authorities through the War Department.

I appeal to all loyal citizens to favor, facilitate, and aid this effort to maintain the honor, the integrity, and the existence of our National Union, and the perpetuity of popular Government, and to redress wrongs already long enough endured.

I deem it proper to say that the first service assigned to the forces hereby called forth will probably be to repossess the forts, places, and property which have been seized from the Union ; and in every event the utmost care will be observed, consistently with the objects aforesaid, to avoid any devastation, any destruction of or interference with property, or any disturbance of peaceful citizens in any part of the country.

And I hereby command the persons composing the combinations aforesaid to disperse and retire peaceably to their respective abodes within twenty days from this date.

Deeming that the present condition of public affairs presents an extraordinary occasion, I do hereby, in virtue of the power in me vested by the Constitution, convene both Houses of Congress.

Senators and Representatives are therefore summoned to assemble at their respective Chambers, at 12 o'clock, noon, on Thursday, the fourth day of July next, then and there to consider and determine such measures as, in their wisdom, the public safety and interest may seem to demand.

In witness whereof, I have hereunto set my hand, and caused the seal of the United States to be affixed.

Done at the city of Washington, this fifteenth day of April, in the year of our Lord one thousand eight hundred and sixty-one, and of the Independence of the United States the eighty-fifth.

[L. S.]

ABRAHAM LINCOLN.

By the President :
    WILLIAM H. SEWARD, *Secretary of State.*

Lincoln's Call for 75,000 Volunteers. Library of Congress.

accepted their offer. All understood that North Carolina had taken a stand and civil war was imminent, and an eerie silence gripped dozens of North Carolina towns. Still, many skeptical young men likely had to "see it to believe it," to grasp that war was imminent. One such young man doubted secession would actually happen until the last minute but volunteered "there and then" when persuaded the news was true.[118]

STATE OF NORTH CAROLINA.

A PROCLAMATION,

BY JOHN W. ELLIS,

GOVERNOR OF NORTH CAROLINA

WHEREAS: By Proclamation of Abraham Lincoln, President of the United States, followed by a requisition of Simon Cameron, Secretary of War, I am informed that the said Abraham Lincoln has made a call for 75,000 men to be employed for the invasion of the peaceful homes of the South, and for the violent subversion of the liberties of a free people, constituting a large part of the whole population of the late United States: And, whereas, this high-handed act of tyrannical outrage is not only in violation of all constitutional law, in utter disregard of every sentiment of humanity and Christian civilization, and conceived in a spirit of aggression unparalleled by any act of recorded history, but is a direct step towards the subjugation of the whole South, and the conversion of a free Republic, inherited from our fathers, into a military despotism, to be established by worse than foreign enemies on the ruins of our once glorious Constitution of Equal Rights.

Now, therefore, I, JOHN W. ELLIS, Governor of the State of North-Carolina, for these extraordinary causes, do hereby issue this, my Proclamation, notifying and requesting the Senators and Members of the House of Commons of the General Assembly of North-Carolina, to meet in Special Session at the Capitol, in the City of Raleigh, on Wednesday the first day of May next. And I furthermore exhort all good citizens throughout the State to be mindful that their first allegiance is due to the Sovereignty which protects their homes and dearest interests, as their first service is due for the sacred defence of their hearths, and of the soil which holds the graves of our glorious dead.

United action in defence of the sovereignty of North-Carolina, and of the rights of the South, becomes now the duty of all.

Given under my hand, and attested by the Great Seal of the State. Done at the City of Raleigh, the 17th day of April, A. D., 1861, and in the eighty-fifth year of our Independence,

JOHN. W. ELLIS.

By the Governor,
GRAHAM DAVES, *Private Secretary*.

Governor John W. Ellis' Response to Lincoln's Call for 75,000 Volunteers.
Library of Congress.

The silence was soon broken when several artillery companies across the state boomed out a celebratory battery fire to announce that war had finally come.[119]

That afternoon, when the governor's call for volunteers was announced in Raleigh, several volunteer companies received new orders to report to the North Carolina coast. Captain Francis McNeely of the Rowan Rifle Guards hastily called the company together and announced that their mission was to "assist the militia in forming a garrison of Fort Caswell in Brunswick County."[120]

The state was buzzing with excitement. Observing the transition from unionist to secessionist loyalties, the editor of the *Carolina Watchman*, John Brunner, reflected that when the townspeople finally recognized that "war was inevitable," he felt burdened to persuade them to "wholeheartedly" support the war effort.[121]

Citizens quickly mobilized to support the effort, as one group of ladies began making "caps of North Carolina cloth" for the soldiers. Just after sunrise on April 21, three companies from Rowan and Cabarrus Counties had just left their homes upon hearing the martial sound of fife and drums calling them to muster for the trip to Fort Caswell on the North Carolina coast. The Cabarrus Guards and Cabarrus Rifles tendered their services to the state on April 18, 1861, and later became Companies A and D, respectively, 20th NCST.[122]

The Rowan Rifles, who were preparing to board the trains for Wilmington, watched as Private James Bowers proudly bore their new silk flag. The company created an imposing sight, as they waited in formation wearing their fancy dress blue uniform coats and caps. The *Carolina Watchman* recorded their departure on that crisp morning of April 23, 1861, as they moved toward Fort Caswell,

DEPARTURE OF TROOPS

The Rowan Rifle Guard, accompanied by the Cabarrus Guard, and the Cabarrus Black Boys, and the Iredell Blues, left this place on Sunday morning for Fort Caswell, below Wilmington. An immense concourse of citizens assembled at the depot to witness the departure. It was an impressive scene. The men seemed resolute and determined, and will no doubt give a good account of themselves when service is required of them.

By appointment the Rowan Rifle Guard assembled at the Methodist Church Saturday evening for prayer, and also at the Presbyterian Church, at 7 o'clock, Sunday morning. After the services at the latter place, they marched to the music of the Salisbury Band to the depot. There they took leave of their friends; and being joined by the above companies, all proceeded on the same train.[123]

As the troops deployed, secession fever pitched in the state amidst a flurry of political rhetoric. The *Salisbury Banner* editorialized their new allegiance on April 23, 1861,

EXCITING TIMES

Our town has been in unusual excitement for the last week, which has resulted in unity of feeling, unity of heart, and firm determined purpose and unwavering spirit of resistance against the Huns and Vandals of the North, who have dared menace our Liberty and domestic peace.

Our people are one in sentiment, in interest, and all agree that the time has come, when we should rally as one man in defense of our liberty, our homes, our firesides, our wives and our children. And not only here, but the people of the county—the State, so far was we have been able to hear, have caught the contagious flame and are elamorous to be led forth to vindicate their ancient honor and the glory of their cause.

Lincoln may raise his millions of blood-thirsty mercenaries, but this Spartan spirit of resistance to an unholy, ungodly, and unlawful disposition of power, that animates the hearts of our brave, united people, will never be crushed until he shall have gained such a victory....

Yea! it will be crushed when the brave sons of North Carolina and of the South shall have been silenced by the cold hand of death and found a soldier's grave. But Sunday was, however, the solemn day. The lovely morning was ushered in by martial music and the gathering of men clad in the panoply of war.

At an early hour our streets were crowded with anxious spectators and rarely, if ever has there been so much excitement and bustle in our town since the days our fathers struck for their freedom and threw off the tyrannical yoke of George the III.

About 6 o'clock the Rowan Rifle Guards formed in rank, on the old Courthouse hill, and marched to the Presbyterian Church for prayer. After which they repaired to the depot here the train was in readiness to bear them to the scene of strife. A large concourse of people had gathered here to bid them God speed in so noble a cause and utter silent prayers that they might soon return victorious to the bosoms of their families.

The cars moved off amid the loud booming of cannon, the shouts of the multitude, and waving of handkerchiefs, and hats.... Once en route, the young men, several of whom had never before traveled far from their homes, found that the excitement had spread statewide. They also learned that the prospect of war could also mean a great deal of attention, especially from young ladies.[124]

This attention was much different than the sort they had previously experienced at dances or other social functions where they seemed to have to work much harder and display more self-control.

One soldier observed while riding on the train,

> ...the wildest and most intense greeted us at every point. The waving of handkerchiefs, the smiles of ladies, the throwing of bouquets and the continuous cheering made the scene a grand ovation all along the route and was well calculated to inspire us with unbounded enthusiasm.[125]

Truly, the new volunteers were "embued with the spirit of war that filled the land, and few understood its' tragedy" wrote a young lady watching her brother depart with the Iredell Blues from Statesville, North Carolina, on April 21, 1861. It was the last time she ever saw him.[126]

Iredell Blues, circa 1860. Courtesy North Carolina State Archives.

Captain Absalom K. Simonton, Iredell Blues, circa 1850s. Courtesy Fred Taylor.

CHAPTER SEVEN

SOLDIER LIFE AT FORT CASWELL AND FORT JOHNSTON IN 1861

Five volunteer companies arrived at Fort Caswell to reinforce the militia on April 22, 1861. The *Carolina Watchman* reported on April 30, 1861, that the "Rowan Rifle Guard are posted at Fort Caswell, for the present. Packages for them, left at McCubbins' and Fosters' Store, will be duly forwarded."

Local supporters and concerned citizens routinely collected foodstuffs and blankets for the men at Fort Caswell. The Rowan Rifles and two Cabarrus companies were reassigned to nearby Fort Johnston at Smithville in early May, although the exact date is unknown. The Rowan Rifles and the Cabarrus Guards were the first two companies to reach Fort Johnston; the garrison commander, Capt. J.B. Jones of Cabarrus County, ordered the Rowan Rifles to pitch their tents along a brick walkway underneath the shade of several cedar trees near the water.

Meanwhile, the Cabarrus Guards made their quarters inside the enlisted men's barracks, and the other unit from Concord, North Carolina, the Cabarrus Rifles, were housed in the government hospital located only a few blocks away at the corner of Nash and Howe streets in Smithville. That small hospital building was leased for "one ear of Indian Corn" per year.[127]

Those early days on the North Carolina coast illustrate not only the enlisted soldiers' naïveté but also, on occasion, their officers'. During that time in 1861, the excited volunteers soon learned that camp life and soldiering were a great deal more work than colorful parades and the cheers of adoring young ladies.

Meshack Franklin Hunt, Rowan Rifle Guards, circa 1859–1861. University of North Carolina, Wilson Library.

SOLDIER LIFE AT FORT CASWELL AND FORT JOHNSTON IN 1861

Many officers garrisoning Fort Caswell were only recently elected and only a few had any experience drilling an infantry company much less a battalion sized organization with two or more companies maneuvering at once. Though some had formerly served in the militia or volunteer artillery, they now spent hours poring over the infantry drill manual, written by General William Hardee in 1858, to give the proper commands to their men.[128]

The men also endured much more stern discipline and physical labor in the early coastal garrison than is normally presumed; and, because it preceded even the Camps of Instruction established at Garysburg in July 1861, it was where many volunteers first tasted the rudiments of army life and established their foundations for unit morale, discipline, and cohesion. Those factors would later play a key role in their service across the coming war.

Early garrison life at Fort Caswell and Fort Johnston in 1861 closely resembled a "plebe system," the traditional basic indoctrination program for new cadets at a U.S. military academy, only with more manual labor. Modern plebe training typically lasts a year and is quite rigid; it requires several hours of physical, academic, and disciplinary training each day. Some of the men wrote home to complain, which, in turn, prompted their families to write letters to Governor John Ellis appealing for him to order the officers to relax the discipline, but most simply kept their miseries to themselves.

For example, young men from wealthy families who had never worked a day of hard physical labor in their lives were required to provide 8-9 hours a day of manual labor, hauling sand and dirt onto the parapets of the forts or otherwise strengthening the defenses. This was not something they were accustomed to and several complained bitterly they were reduced to manual laborers instead of being treated as gentlemen.

On the other hand, while some subtly complained or alluded to discomforts in their early letters from the coast, the majority of the volunteers were so enamored with whatever naive concepts of war they had formed by listening to grandparents who were veterans of the Revolution and War of 1812 or by reading books that many of them would do anything to prove themselves worthy of being called "soldiers."

Private George Deal of the Cabarrus Guards wrote home to his sweetheart, Miss Catie Sloop of Rowan County on May 25, 1861, from Fort Johnston. Deal was from Rowan County also, and shows himself to be something of a poet as well as a soldier, as the following letter demonstrates:

> Dear Miss Catie,
>
> We are still at Fort Johnston doing the best we can to enjoy ourselves but at best it is quite little our enjoyment is nothing to compare with our enjoyment at home in old Rowan, where we are among friends and with them that we love and is near and dear unto us. It would give me more pleasure to be in your Company one short week than all the pleasure I will see hear or have seen since I have been home.
>
> If I can't sleep, I wander off the sands of the Eastern Shores and sit down upon the beach of the great Atlantic and hear not a sound but rushing of the mighty waves as they lash under my feet. Fancy carries me back to Old Rowan where all my friends and my memory rest.
>
> My Dear Miss Catie wishing to recall back those happy moments that we have spent in each other's company, but those days have fled for a short period, but I hope that this now disturbed nation will soon become an independent southern Confederacy and we will be returned to our homes and friends in peace that we have left behind…[129]

Another soldier, Private James Lilly of the Wilmington Light Infantry wrote home from Fort Caswell with details of his newfound daily routine, which was to awaken around 5:00 a.m., report to roll call on the parade field, return to his quarters and wash up, that is, if he could find an open basin, a process that he complained could take up to thirty minutes - then return to the parade field again.[130]

The troops at Fort Caswell and Fort Johnston were further required to answer roll call once more before marching to the "mess," or dining area. Each meal was regimented, as serving lines moved in formation, and each company sat at designated tables. If they were late, the troops simply missed their chance to sit at a table and eat. Instead, the latecomers had to "sit on the bricks" outside and wait their turn. The fare usually consisted of rice, bacon, and bread.[131]

SOLDIER LIFE AT FORT CASWELL AND FORT JOHNSTON IN 1861

Fort Caswell, Oak Island, North Carolina. North and Westward view of the parade ground. Barracks and officer's quarters lined the field during the 1861 garrison. Courtesy North Carolina Baptist Convention. Photo by R.C. Hatfield.

Quite possibly, the men were so hungry that even such simple food seemed a delicacy to them. As one volunteer noted, "Our work gives us a good appetite." The daylong hard physical labor performed by the volunteers ended with yet another roll call on the parade ground, then "such scrambling to get to sleep you never saw."[132]

Literally, the soldier's entire day was fully accounted for. When they weren't performing manual labor, the usual fare was to drill throughout the day. They were also required to study both infantry and artillery manuals of arms, something most of the volunteers had not done during their antebellum years. One exception was the Rowan Rifles who had regularly drilled with their sister company, the Rowan Artillery.

Unidentified Rowan Artillery Officer, circa late 1850s. Courtesy Lamar Williams.

It was not unusual to find men from each company switching roles to learn both artillery and infantry tactics during their antebellum years. Ironically, the Rowan Artillery later became Battery D, 10th NCT. That regiment was eventually commanded by none other than the former U.S. Army Ordnance Sergeant James Reilly, who garrisoned Fort Caswell in January and April 1861 when the militia captured the fort. Reilly went on to become a Colonel and led Confederate forces at the final defense of Fort Fisher in February 1865.

SOLDIER LIFE AT FORT CASWELL AND FORT JOHNSTON IN 1861

One private in the Wilmington Light Infantry described their daily regimen at Fort Caswell, "At 8 after breakfast we are drilled until night, resting at short-times every hour or so. If we are not drilled at the cannons, we are drilled at the sea beach with our muskets." He reflected both his pride and naiveté when he wrote home, "I am now a regular solider...wishing to fight for the south & old NC in particular, I gloried in shouldering my rifle. I belonged to my company for a month."[133]

As additional volunteer companies poured into the garrison, conditions became crowded at both facilities. By mid-May, five companies were stationed at Fort Johnston including the Rowan Rifle Guards, the two Cabarrus companies, the Sampson Rangers, the Columbus Guards, and the Duplin Grays. Soon the garrison was over 350 men strong. Many of the officers had not even yet received their official confirmation of commission into state service when they arrived on the coast. Notice that they were officially recognized as state officers did not arrive until June 27, 1861.[134]

Colonel B. R. Moore, commanding the 63d Militia Regiment, traveled to the coast to visit the garrison and reported to the *Carolina Watchman* on April 30, 1861, that "the troops sent to Forts Caswell...are dependent...for bacon, meal, flour, corn, peas, etc. These articles are being gathered...and will be sent...free of charge."

As nearly 400 troops from across the state had now arrived at Fort Caswell, many citizens in their hometowns had little confidence in the militia who remained behind to protect them. The city of Salisbury, North Carolina, formed a "Vigilante Committee" whom they tasked to "patrol anywhere they please." This posse's mission was to patrol streets after dark, carrying one gun, with authority to arrest "suspicious characters that may be lurking about" seeking to make mischief. By August 1, 1861, more reasonable city leaders curtailed this somewhat extreme reaction, and the group was disbanded.[135]

Routine garrison life at Fort Caswell and Fort Johnston was occasionally interrupted by visitation from soldiers' wives and children who commonly traveled to and from Smithville on various steamers to see their loved ones in these early weeks of the War. As the fledgling soldiers settled into their strict new routine, frequent formal military ceremonies and an officious demeanor was the order of the day at both Fort Caswell and Fort Johnston.[136]

TREASON ON THE CAPE FEAR

View of Fort Caswell, on West Side of Cape Fear River.
Frank Leslie's Illustrated Newspaper, March 4, 1865. Library of Congress.

Coastal Artillery en Barbette similar to Fort Caswell 1861. Library of Congress.

SOLDIER LIFE AT FORT CASWELL AND FORT JOHNSTON IN 1861

An unidentified soldier published a letter to the citizens of Salisbury in the *Carolina Watchman* on May 1, 1861, describing their activities at Fort Johnston. The ceremony was led by Captain Francis "Frank" McNeeley, a former member of the Rowan Artillery. He took command as follows,

> I suppose you would like to hear occasionally from the Rowan Rifle Guard. Of course our time for correspondence is quite limited, but I steal a few moments to inform you of the high distinction conferred upon our beautiful flag.
>
> This being 1st of May, at ten minutes before nine o'clock, our battalion was paraded upon the green in front of the barracks, where a pole, eighty feet high, had been erected by order of our commander, Capt. J.P. [J.B.] Jones of the Confederate Army.
>
> A 9 o'clock, precisely, the flag of the Rowan Rifle Guards was ordered to the front where it was received by Mr. J. Mc L. Turner, who bored it to the pole, the battalion presented arms, and when our boys saw it floating high in the breeze, proudly waving above them, they stood gazing upon it in silent admiration, every heart was swelling, every eye was beaming, and every thought was of home, of Rowan, lovely glorious old Rowan, her green hills and her greener forests; above all, they thought of those fair hands that combined that beautiful Sabbath morning when they bade them farewell.
>
> There was no mistaking that common feeling, it was written upon every face, eloquent in every eye, they were proud of their flag, proud of their kindred, their country, and their cause. But if the sons of Rowan were proud of their flag, their comrades in arms were not less so; the brave sons of Cabarrus, our kindred, and our neighbors, were there to do homage to our flag, theirs ere not the sisters not that wrought it, but theirs was the cause.
>
> They saw there the star they worshipped, that single star, the emblem of North Carolina's untarnished fame. It was an inspiring sight. All combined to heighten the effect. In the distance the eye traced the white beach, girt with those terrible breakers, whose foaming crests can never permit the advancing mermindons of Lincoln to invade the hallowed soil of North Carolina, while upon the point of the beach that borders the channel, Fort

Caswell frowned, jealous and watchful—the advancing tide with its measured cadence swept along the shell strewed beach.

The sun shone brightly as we have so often seen the May sun brighten the green hills of Rowan. And this was all part and parcel of North Carolina—our own loved State. And few were the hearts in that line of volunteer soldiers that did not swell with devotion to her honor and her interests.

The flag lingered awhile aloft, it's beautiful folds reflected from the restless waters of the Cape Fear, then slowly descended. As it neared the earth, the artillery belched forth its thunders, Capt. McNeely of our company firing the first gun, nine guns were fired when Capt. McNeely received it and returned it to the Ensign. Thus was our flag honored.

Many times again I trust we will honor it, should Lincoln ever dare to invade our beloved State, or her sisters of the sunny South. Her sons are brave and determined. Today the boat brought us a quantity of tents, provisions clothing &c., from our considerate friends at home, and as long as they display this spirit of liberality and tender regard for the welfare of the company, we were the worst of ingrates did we not strive to reflect credit upon our country.

We are well provided for in every way and all our men are cheerful and contented; sternly determined to see the close of the dawn. We see the Watchman occasionally and I assure you it revives many tender memories of home.[137]

Exceptional zeal does not make one a skilled soldier, however, as a seventeen-year-old private soon learned. A lack of knowledge could be equally as dangerous as a lack of heavy artillery at Fort Caswell.

The following event occurred as the volunteer companies were streaming into the fort on April 22, 1861,

> To illustrate the utter ignorance of us all, officers and men, of what we most needed to know at the time, Company A was ordered to assist in mounting some guns in Fort Caswell. The first one we attacked was an eight-inch Columbiad a huge piece of metal which we were to roll up to the nearby perpendicular embankment to the parapet and lift to its place on the gun carriage.

With our crude devices and inexperience, it was a Herculean task, but at last we accomplished it and were very proud of our job.

The next morning at sunrise our squad was detailed to fire the morning gun from our piece, the only one at that time mounted in the fort. The gunner pulled his lanyard, the great piece belched forth its thunder and for an infinitesimal moment we were much delighted with its great noise.

But the recoil that always follows a firing caused the gun carriage to tilt up and the infernal thing went end over end to the foot of the embankment. No one bethought them to place where it belonged, the "prop" (an integral part of the gun carriage then in use and designed to prevent just what had happened)....[138]

Typical of inexperienced soldiers, rumors also soon abounded of a coming assault on their position. A young private in the Iredell Blues, John Stikeleather, who hailed from Statesville, North Carolina, recalled an incident further demonstrating the green volunteers' inexperience when they arrived at Fort Caswell.

The reader should bear in mind, however, that Stikeleather wrote about the occurrence years after the war. At that point in his life, the early coastal events seemed ridiculous to him given the horrors of combat and four years of privation he subsequently experienced on active campaigns.

Yet, Stikeleather reveals that to most of the new soldiers, the perceived threat on the North Carolina coast was quite real in 1861:

...the turbulence of the waves today and their placid shimmer at sunrise tomorrow, the bathing in the vast Atlantic, the hurrying away from an imaginary shark, the drilling, picketing, and watching out for an incoming war steamer and other things not necessary to mention, were well calculated to prevent an attack of ennui for a few weeks at least.

Some four or five other companies besides ours were at the fort similarly engaged. An incident or two illustrative of the ludicrous side of soldier life occurs to memory here, by the way how fortunate it is that there is a ludicrous side to war, but for the fact, many now at home, useful citizens, a comfort, and support to their friends, never would have survived the terrible ordeal through which they passed in the late war.

One of the incidents occurred on picket. At Fort Caswell we remained for some four weeks, drilling, and perfecting our organization. We western boys enjoyed the scenery along the seacoast with a keen zest, the broad expanse of water. A heavy guard was required to picket the seacoast for several miles below the fort day and night to warn the garrison of the approach of a war steamer or anything else of a suspicious nature. False alarms were frequent as might have been expected of an inexperienced soldiery.

The shooting of a star, the firing of a musket, and such like occurrences resulted several times in arousing our soldiers from their peaceful slumbers, much to their chagrin after they became satisfied the alarm was false. I very well remember being on picket one night on the coast. The line of pickets that night was perhaps two miles long, and the number of pickets in charge of a commissioned officer about thirty.

My beat was near the water's edge on hard white sand from which the tide had receded but a few hours before. Our respective beats were about one hundred yards each, and the instructions were, that should anything suspicious be seen or heard, the one making the discovery was to immediately fire off his gun as an alarm to the entire line, which was to be at once followed by the firing of every picket on duty.

Then the pickets were to leave their beats and assemble at the point where the first gun was fired to ascertain the cause of the alarm and arouse the garrison. On the night alluded to an Irishman was on the beat on my immediate left; as we passed back and forth we frequently accosted each other to help wile away the hours.

Just before midnight I noticed a light appearance in the east, and was congratulating myself that I was about to witness what I had never seen before, namely, a moonrise on the Atlantic. As the brightness increased in the eastern horizon and I was getting ready to break forth in exclamation of delight at the beautiful, and to me, unusual scene of a moonrise on the water, my friend the Irishman just on my left, called to me to fire off my gun.

I asked him why, pointing to what I had supposed was the rising moon, he said Look at that war steamer coming in, she will open fire upon the fort in a few minutes, I told him my impressions were otherwise, but he said he had been there long before and knew the difference in a war steamer and a moonrise after night.

I was still somewhat skeptical in regard to his theory of the phenomenon being correct, and was loath to relinquish the idea of witnessing a moonrise on the ocean, but thought I might possibly be mistaken.

However, I remarked to my friend the Irishman, that was we were together that I would save my load, and if he was sure the light we saw was the blaze and smoke of a war steamer to fire off his musket, and he did so; pop, pop, pop, up and down the line, and the pickets in a few moments with the officer of the night came running up from right and left to find the cause of the alarm. The chagrin of my friend the Irishman can be imagined when I state that the moon (for moon it was) had got clean up out of the water and was hanging there in all its silvery brightness almost before any inquiry could be made by the officer of the pickets at all in regard to the alarm.

By this time the garrison of the fort had been aroused and were out on the parapet awaiting an immediate attack. My gun was loaded, the only one loaded on the line after the alarm till the pickets reloaded. In a little while everything resumed its former status. Paddy discovered no more war steamers during our stay at the fort.[139]

Other than sore legs from drilling all day, there were not a significant number of medical problems during the first days of active service at Fort Caswell. Yet, many acquired unhealthy habits as a popular, albeit erroneous, belief was that in order to ward off sickness one had only to take up smoking, but tobacco was also quite difficult to acquire at that location.[140]

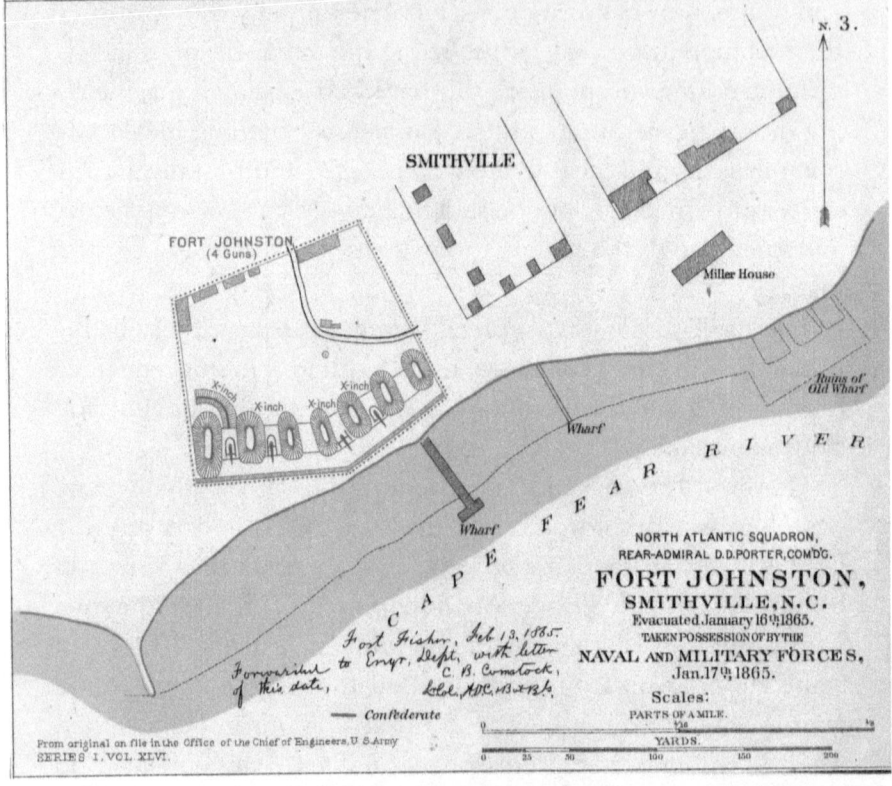

New Hanover Library Local History Room.

On May 2, 1861, the *Carolina Watchman* indicated the morale there was strong, and also confirmed that the Rowan Rifles were still at Fort Johnston. Notice the author also provides us with more insight as to the identity of the post commander, Capt. J.B. Jones,

FROM THE CAPE FEAR

It is gratifying to watch the rapidity with which the martial spirit of the Old North State is developing. But a few weeks ago all was quiet within her borders; now, from mountain to ocean, we hear the onward tramp of thousands of her devoted sons, who have left their homes to meet the invaders of her hallowed soil.

But more especially, do we listen with eager interest for tidings from the mouth of the Cape Fear, here are stationed our kindred and friends, and we are gratified to announce upon the authority of a gentleman just returned from Fort Johnston, that the troops, stationed at that place, are rapidly improving, and will soon reach the point of efficiency, when it will be dangerous for the hirelings of the North to encounter them.

Our informant represents the men as contented and light hearted, but at the same time resolute and determined. Many of them, we know well, for among them, we recognize the sons of Cabarrus, descendants of the first champions in the first war of independence.

They are now side by side with the Rowan Rifle Guard, and side by side may they stand till the great work is accomplished. The commander at Fort Johnston is Capt. J.P. [J.B.] Jones, an officer of considerable experience, having held commission in the United States Army. Upon the commencement of the two sections, he resigned and accepted one in the Confederate Army.

He was in command of a battery at the bombardment of Sumpter. He is, we learn, a strict disciplinarian, but at the same time highly popular with his command, both officers and privates.

We already have a strong force at the mouth of the Cape Fear, and recruits are daily pouring in. Let Mr. Lincoln send some of his holiday soldiery around by that way and take our word for it, they will open their eyes as to the men they have to deal with.[141]

Another significant event soon occurred at Fort Caswell, as the volunteer companies mustered into twelve months' service as state volunteers on May 9, 1861. The next day, the *Carolina Watchman* indicated all was well with the garrison at Fort Caswell, and that the volunteers were electing delegates for the secession convention at Raleigh. Note the "company" refers to the Rowan Rifles, who were then at Fort Johnston,

> A letter from a member of this Company now in Fort Caswell, informs us that all are well and in fine spirits. Nothing of special interest. The vote of the Company was taken for delegates to the convention. Craige and [J.B.] Jones received a majority of the whole number cast, though the vote was very much divided between the other persons.[142]

A few days later, there was another crisis near Smithville, when an unknown cargo ship crept up the Cape Fear River, and the soldiers formed up a boarding party to capture it. An article appeared in the *Carolina Watchman* on May 20, 1861, reprinted from the May 18, 1861 edition of the *Charleston Courier*, indicating the "N. Carolinians became excited, and they have reason to believe she is a government transport...."[143]

The mysterious ship turned out to be the *Thomas Watson* from New York, but her purpose there remained "not yet ascertained" for several days. The article reported that four Rowan Rifles members were among the capture party, including Captain Williams Brown, and three other soldiers. However, Williams Brown was then a first sergeant, not a captain.[144]

On May 20, 1861, the state of North Carolina formally seceded from the United States. An excerpt from North Carolina's Ordinance of Secession follows:

> An Ordinance to dissolve the union between the State of North Carolina and the other States united with her, under the compact of government entitled "The Constitution of the United States."
>
> We, the people of the State of North Carolina in convention assembled, do declare, and ordain, and it is hereby declared and ordained, That the ordinance adopted by the State of North Carolina in the convention of 1789, whereby the Constitution of the United States was ratified and adopted, and also all acts and parts of acts of the General Assembly ratifying and adopting amendments to the said Constitution, are hereby repealed, rescinded, and abrogated.
>
> We do further declare and ordain, That the union now subsisting between the State of North Carolina and the other States, under the title of the United States of America, is hereby dissolved, and that the State of North Carolina is in full possession and exercise of all those rights of sovereignty which belong and appertain to a free and independent State....[145]

After hearing the news, the garrison troops boasted of their devotion to their state. The Rowan Rifles published their own declaration on May 23, 1861, in the *Carolina Watchman*:

> Dear Watchman:
>
> At a meeting of the Rowan Rifle Guards, held at this camp on Saturday the 18th of May 1861, Capt. F.M.Y. McNeely was invited to take the chair, and H.C. Long was to act as Secretary, when the following resolutions were read and unanimously passed.
>
> Resolved 1st. That we hereby tender the citizens of Rowan County our earnest acknowledgements of the debt of gratitude which we owe them for the promptness and liberality with which they have contributed to relieve the wants of the Company, called upon in an emergency when the forms of the State government could not be exercised with sufficient dispatch, the generous sons of Rowan have responded nobly to the voice of patriotism, and are making sacrifices that we behold in a people whose ardent devotion to liberty, stands paramount over any other passion. Wisdom hath another lesson for those that would conquer them.
>
> Resolved 2d. That in the Ladies of the county we recognize invaluable friends, Judicious in imagining the wants of the Company, they have been as active in relieving them; brave, magnanimous spirits! The recollection of their sacrifices, of their anxious solicitude, and their zeal in the cause of freedom, has inspired within us new pride for our kindred, and thrown an additional tenderness around the memory of home. To them we tender our thanks and venture the hope, that the sequel may prove that they have not bestowed their kindness upon soldiers less resolute than themselves.[146]

CHAPTER EIGHT

A TIME FOR WAR

The North Carolina Revised Militia Code of 1854 did not require volunteer companies with fewer than sixty-four men and officers to file an annual muster roll with the state adjutant general's office, although officers requesting weapons from the state arsenal were required to post a bond "of sufficient security" for the weapons in the governor's office.[147]

If the company was ever mustered into state service, that law provided the governor an option of filling gaps in the volunteer companies ranks with men from the state militia, those same undisciplined fellows who usually viewed drill and muster only as a social event. On May 27, 1861, Colonel John F. Hoke, then the Adjutant General of North Carolina, reported to Governor John Ellis that he was aware of the "... the number of volunteers that have tendered their services to the State and... the number of troops stationed at each post in the State."

Hoke also told Ellis that, "The exact number of men belonging to each company, except those mustered into service, cannot be ascertained. The companies tendered have each sixty-four men rank and file. Muster rolls have been forwarded to the different places where troops have been ordered to assemble, and the complete muster rolls will be forwarded to this office." According to Hoke, several of the volunteers at Fort Caswell and Fort Johnston had not yet forwarded a muster roll to his office on May 27, 1861.[148]

Another letter written the same date by Warren Winslow to the Honorable Weldon N. Edwards, chairman of the 1861 North Carolina Convention, shows that the governor was virtually uninformed as to the actual whereabouts of the volunteer companies, although several were already deployed to the coastal areas.

Except for some companies already assigned to the 1st, 2d, 4th, 5th, 6th, and 7th NCST regiments (who were then forming in camps near Raleigh), most volunteer companies were in a kind of limbo during this period and left little, if any, official records of their activities. Winslow indicated those units whose location and activities were known by the state were only ascertained by inference from general correspondence, not from actual muster rolls in the adjutant general's office.

Private Alfred Turner, Company C, "The Saltillo Boys," 4th North Carolina State Troops, circa 1861. University of North Carolina Library, Chapel Hill.

Winslow, like Colonel John F. Hoke, also reported that he could not yet accurately report the rendezvous location or strength of the volunteer companies deployed to the field, as he had no muster rolls or even enlistment documents for any officers, non-commissioned officers, or enlisted men yet on file.

Winslow, although dependent upon Hoke's office for information, clearly did not indulge himself in intradepartmental politics but rather practical necessity, when he further complained on May 24, 1861, that "Until all the troops are mustered into the service, the number of privates and non-commissioned officers, the latter of whom are appointed by the Colonels respectively, cannot be ascertained....Not a single commission has been issued to any officer of a Regiment."[149]

There had simply not been enough time to gather the needed information from the various garrisons on the coast of North Carolina with hundreds of new volunteers added each week. But a lack of time was not the only reason that many of the companies at Fort Caswell and Fort Johnston did not file a muster roll; Hoke again wrote to Ellis on June 24, 1861, with a composite report of the location, officers, and number of men in each volunteer company then deployed to the field from North Carolina.

Fort Johnston Officers' Quarters circa 1900.
Courtesy Lower Cape Fear Historical Society.

In this report, Hoke indicated that the total garrison at Fort Johnston then contained five volunteer companies with 18 officers, 38 non-commissioned officers, and 324 privates inside the fort. Two other volunteer companies stationed there had already completed and returned their muster rolls, including two from Cabarrus County, who were reported as then part of the "10th Regiment NC Militia" along with the Rowan Rifle Guards and other companies.[150]

However, Hoke stated further to Ellis that "...no record is kept of companies not having the full complement of men," referencing the 1854 militia law that did not require volunteer companies with fewer than 64 men (including commissioned officers) to file muster rolls in the adjutant general's office.

The Rowan Rifles were ordered to the coast on April 22, 1861, but as of June 24, 1861, Captain Frank McNeely had not filed a muster roll with the adjutant general, making it impossible to know exactly how many troops first deployed to garrison Fort Caswell and Fort Johnston from April to May 1861. By June 1861, however, hundreds of new volunteers formed companies, and many were deployed to forts along the Cape Fear.

At Fort Caswell, Colonel John Cantwell then commanded a battalion comprised of the Cape Fear Light Artillery, Rifle Rangers, Fair Bluff Volunteers, Columbus Guards, Wilmington Volunteers and the Iredell Blues. At nearby Fort Caswell then also hosted the Cabarrus Blackboys, Rowan Rifle Guards, Sampson Rangers, with Company No. 4 of the Columbus Guards, and Captain C.G. Dennison's company from Duplin County. Two companies of the Bladen Guards [Bladen Volunteers] and the Cape Fear Rifles were posted at Wilmington as well, while the Wilmington Light Infantry were transferred to Federal Point, and the Brunswick Guards were sent to Lockwood's Folly.[151]

The Rowan Rifles were typical of volunteer companies in North Carolina during the early war period, with between 60-64 men present on May 30, 1861, when they mustered into service. That number was below the benchmark of sixty-four men set by the Revised North Carolina Militia Law of 1860. This potentially explains the general lack of official muster rolls or other records during this formative era or it could simply have been due to the officer' inexperience. There were no deaths due to illness, wounds, or accidental injuries reported at Fort

Caswell or Fort Johnston from April to June 1861, so those factors did not affect the garrison.[152]

Private William H. Rockwell, Co. H, 8th North Carolina Volunteers, circa 1861. Library of Congress.

From analysis of later muster rolls and other military records of those companies, we can form a general, but realistic sketch of the typical volunteer's physical appearance at Fort Johnston and Fort Caswell in April 1861. The average enlisted man was between the ages 17 and 21 years, with 33% aged 22 to 25 years; and only a few were older than 30 years.

The majority were unmarried, and their usual occupation was as a farmer or farm laborer, although some were also brick masons, carpenters, clerks, and tinsmiths. A popular modern narrative asserts that all Confederate officers were elite, wealthy slaveholders, and the enlisted men were poor farmers with no slaves. However, according to the 1860 U.S. Census, none of the officers in the Rowan Rifle Guards owned slaves, although most of their families did. On the other hand, roughly 8% of the enlisted men held slaves, most of whom were subleased as laborers at the Gold Hill mines near Salisbury.[153]

Archibald Daniel Council, Bladen Guards, circa 1861.
(Later became Co. K, 18th NCT) Library of Congress.

A TIME FOR WAR

The volunteers garrisoning Fort Johnston mustered into service for three years or the duration of the war on May 30, 1861, at Smithville. While awaiting new orders, the soldiers were acutely aware that they would soon be reassigned into one of the new state regiments then forming near Raleigh, while most of the militia from the Wilmington area planned on staying along the coast. Several of the companies sent delegations back home to recruit men to fill their ranks. One volunteer officer was actively working through political channels "trying to procure a position" from state officials for his company in one of the newly forming State Regiments."[154]

By July 1, 1861, most of the volunteer companies at Fort Caswell and Fort Johnston had received news they were ordered to Garysburg, North Carolina, to begin Camp of Instruction; however, Colonel John Cantwell's militia stayed behind, and the Wilmington Light Infantry were sent across the channel to Federal Point where they began constructing earthworks for Fort Fisher at Battery Bolles in July.

Rebel works on the Cape Fear River, near Wilmington, North Carolina. *Frank Leslie's Illustrated Newspaper*, March 18, 1865. Library of Congress.

111

One of the soldiers in the Wilmington Rifle Guards, Private James I. Metts, was formerly a student at the University of North Carolina. He found the rigid military discipline quite miserable, and often wrote to his family grousing of it. His dislike was so strong that his mother eventually advised that perhaps he should "reenlist as an independent volunteer."[155]

James Isaac Metts, Wilmington Rifle Guards, circa 1861. Lt. William Penn Metts, Newbern Light Infantry, and he were cousins. The Wilmington Rifle Guards became Co. I, 8th North Carolina Volunteers and 18th NCT. Courtesy North Carolina State Archives.

Governor John Ellis was at that time in very poor health. His doctors recommended he travel to Red Sulphur Springs, Virginia (now Mercer County, West Virginia) hoping the sulfur baths would improve his condition; it did not, and he died on July 7, 1861.[156]

Unidentified Southern Volunteer circa 1861. Library of Congress.

The early volunteers' naïve impressions of a glorious war formed during antebellum was a great contrast to "sojering" in the relatively safe coastal garrison not far from their homes. Yet, this experience paled in contrast to the horrors ahead of them, where they would quickly learn that war was anything but glorious.

Summarily, despite rumors of an impending Federal invasion, the early garrisons posted along the Cape Fear River did not see any action in early 1861. Although the events transpiring there have gone largely unnoticed in the annals of Civil War history, the actions of the North Carolina militia made a direct contribution to the complex chain of events ultimately leading to the American Civil War.

Colonel John Cantwell, commanding the 30th Regiment North Carolina Militia later succinctly summarized events of that turbulent era,

> Thus was war inaugurated in North Carolina more than a month prior to the act of secession, and it is a noteworthy fact that the news of the act dissolving its connection with the Union, and the call upon her sons to arm themselves was first made known to the pioneer troops of the Cape Fear on the parade ground at Fort Caswell.[157]

BIBLIOGRAPHY

Books

Wilson Angley, "*A History of Fort Johnston on the Lower Cape Fear*," (Southport, NC: Southport Historical Society, 1996).

William K. Boyd. *North Carolina on the Eve of Secession*. (Washington, DC: Annual Report of the American Historical Association, 1912).

Stephen Bradley. *North Carolina Militia Officers Roster as Contained in the Adjutant General's Officers Roster*. (Wilmington, NC: Broadfoot Publishing, 1992).

James S. Brawley. *The Rowan Story 1753-1953: A Narrative History of Rowan County, North Carolina*. (Salisbury, North Carolina: Rowan Printing, 1953).

——— *Rowan County: A Brief History*. (Raleigh, NC: NC Department of Archives and History, 1974).

——— *The Carolina Watchman Index*. Original copy held in the Edith M. Clark History Room, Rowan County Library, Salisbury, NC.

Walter Clark, (Ed.), *Histories of the Several Regiments and Battalions from North Carolina in the Great War 1861-1865, Written by Members of the Various Commands*. (Raleigh, NC:1901). Vols. 1-5.

Clayton E. Jewett and John O. Allen. *Slavery in the South: A State-by-State History*. (Westport, Connecticut: Greenwood Press, 2004).

Philip S. Foner. *Business and Slavery: The New York Merchants and the Irrepressible Conflict*. (Chapel Hill, North Carolina: UNC Press, 1942).

Chris E. Fonvielle, Jr. *Faces of Fort Fisher*. (Carolina Beach, NC: Slapdash Publishing, 2013).

Thomas R. Gray. *Confessions of Nat Turner, the Leader of the Late Insurrection in South Hampton, Va.* Original copy in Library of Congress, Call No. F232.S7T9 (Richmond, VA: T.R. Gray, 1832).

Ethel Herring and Carole Williams. *Fort Caswell in War and Peace.* (Wendell, NC: Broadfoot Publishing, 1983)

—— *Fort Caswell in War and Peace.* (Wendell, NC: Broadfoot Publishing, Revised edition, 1999).

Guion G. Johnson. *Antebellum North Carolina: A Social History.* (Chapel Hill, NC: University of North Carolina Press, 1937)

Tim Kearney (Ed.). *Abstracts of Letters of Resignation of Militia Officers in North Carolina 1779-1840.* (Raleigh, NC: Walsworth Printing Company, 1992).

Louis H. Manarin and Weymouth T. Jordan Jr., *North Carolina Troops, 1861-1865: A Roster.* Vols. 1-20. (Raleigh NC: NC Department of Archives & History, 2004).

John B. Moore, (Ed.), *The Works of James Buchanan Comprising his Speeches, State Papers, and Private Correspondence.* Vol. 11, (Philadelphia and London: J.B. Lippincott Co., 1860-1868).

McPherson, James M. *Abraham Lincoln and the Second American Revolution,* (New York, NY: Oxford University Press, 1991).

——*Battle Cry of Freedom.* (New York, NY: Oxford University Press, 2003).

Randall Osborne & Jeffrey C. Weaver, *The Virginia State Rangers and Virginia State Line,* (Lynchburg, VA: H.E. Howard, 1994).

James Sprunt, *Chronicles of the Cape Fear River: 1600-1916.* (Spartanburg, SC, 1974; reprint, Wilmington, NC: Broadfoot Publishing, 1992)

Taylor, Marian. *Harriet Tubman: Antislavery Activist.* (New York, NY: Chelsea House Publishers, 2004), 68-69.

BIBLIOGRAPHY

Noble J. Tolbert, (Ed.). *The Papers of John Willis Ellis.* Vols. 1&2. (Raleigh, NC: NC State Archives, 1964).

James Oakes. *Slavery and Freedom: An Interpretation of the Old South.* (New York, NY: Alfred A. Knopf, 1990).

Ulrich B. Phillips. *Life and Labor in the Old South.* (Columbia, SC: University of South Carolina Press),

William S. Powell. *Dictionary of North Carolina Biography,* Vol. 2., D-G. (Chapel Hill, North Carolina: UNC Press, 1996).

William D. Rawle. *A view of the Constitution of the United States of America.* (Durham, North Carolina: Carolina Academic Press, 2009).

Stampp, Kenneth M. *The Peculiar Institution.* (New York, NY: Vintage Books, 1954).

Manuscripts

Elle M. Andrews. *Elle's Book, Being the Journal Kept by Elle M. Andrews from April 23, 1861, through May 1865.* Transcribed and annotated by Ann Campbell. Held at the Edith M. Clark History Room, Rowan Public Library, Salisbury, North Carolina.

John Lucas Paul Cantwell Papers 1830-1925. Collection No. 03027, Southern Historical Collection, Wilson Library, University of North Carolina at Chapel Hill.

Letter from George Deal, Cabarrus Guards, May 25, 1861, to Miss Catie Sloop of Rowan County. Original held in private collection of George Patterson, Concord, North Carolina. Used with permission.

John Willis Ellis Diary, Transcript. Entries for November 28 & 29, 1860. In J.W. Ellis Papers, 1844-1958. #242 Southern Historical Collection, Coll. No. 00242, Official Papers and Correspondence, 1861, Folder 25. Wilson Library, University of North Carolina, Chapel Hill.

John W. Ells Papers, 1844-1958. #242 Southern Historical Collection, Coll. No. 00242, Official Papers and Correspondence, 1861, pertaining particularly to Secession and the beginning of the Civil War. Wilson Library, University of North Carolina at Chapel Hill.

Fred C. Foard, Civil War Remembrances. North Carolina State Archives, Confederate Papers No. 172, Southern Historical Collection, The Wilson Library, University of North Carolina at Chapel Hill, North Carolina.

James Lilly, Letter to Ms. Catie, from Fort Caswell, May 4, 1861. Private Collections, Miscellaneous Papers, 1689-1912, Lilly Family Papers, 1785-1863. North Carolina Department of Archives and History.

Abraham Lincoln. Abraham Lincoln Papers: Series 2. General Correspondence 1858-1864. Abraham to Horace Greeley. Clipping from the Friday, Aug. 23, 1862, *Daily National Intelligencer*, Washington, D.C. Library of Congress.

John A. Stikeleather, Recollections of the Civil War in the United States 1861-1865. (Olin, N.C.: University of North Carolina Chapel Hill, Southern Historical Collection, May 27, 1909).

Newspapers

Wilmington Daily Herald. Newspaper Reading Room, SN 920739122, Library of Congress.

The Carolina Watchman. Microfilm held in The Edith M. Clark History Room, Rowan County Library, Salisbury, North Carolina.

Statesville Landmark, Newspaper Reading Room, SN85042202, Library of Congress, Washington, D.C.

Periodicals

"The Hedgehog and the Foxes," *Journal of the Abraham Lincoln Association*, Vol. 12(1), (1991), 49-65.

Swanberg, W.A. "Was the Secretary of War a Traitor?" (Feb. 1963), *American Heritage*, Vol. 14(2).

BIBLIOGRAPHY

ONLINE

Cape Fear Historical Institute. www.cfhi.net.

Civil War Era NC, https://cwnc.omeka.chass.ncsu.edu.

Documenting the American South, University of North Carolina Chapel Hill. http://docsouth.unc.edu/nc/goodloe.

Lincoln, Abraham. Abraham Lincoln papers: Series 1. General Correspondence. 1833 to 1916. ID No. MSS30189. Report on Southern Forts. Manuscript-Fixed Material. www.loc.gov/itemma10850000/.

North Carolinians Debate *Secession*, http://lp/editions/nchist-civilwar.

North Carolina Digital Collections, http://digital.ncdcr.gov.

North Carolina Digital History. www.learnnc.org

Secession Era Editorials Project, http://history.furman.edu.

The American Presidency Project, The University of California, Santa Barbara, http://www.presidency.ucsb.edu.

Wilmington Journal. https://chroniclingamerican.loc.gov.

Wilmington Daily Herald, Secession Era Editorials Project. http://history.furman.edu.

Wilmington Daily Herald, https: chroniclingamerica.loc.gov.

GOVERNMENT PUBLICATIONS

Civil War Collection: Regimental Records, Muster Rolls of North Carolina State Troops 1861-1865, Co. K, 4th NCST. AG-16, Box 48, December 31, 1861. North Carolina Department of Archives and History.

Compiled Military Service Records, Confederate. RG 95, M324. Microfilm held at The Edith M. Clark History Room, Rowan Public Library, Salisbury, North Carolina.

Confederate States of America Documents, 1861-1865, MSS16550, Box 34, Reels 36& 37, Library of Congress.

Federal Writer's Project: Slave Narrative Project, Vol. 11, North Carolina, Part 2, Jackson-Yellerday. (1936). Manuscript/Mixed Material, (Washington, DC: 1941, Library of Congress).

Militia Act of 1792, Second Congress, Session 1. Chapter 28, Second Act, Article 1, ss. 1-5(i). Passed May 2, 1792. Printed Ephemera Collection, Portfolio 222, Folder 13, Library of Congress.

North Carolina Convention & Military Board 1861-1862, Original held at North Carolina Collection, Call No. VC342.2 1861d Vol. 1, University of North Carolina at Chapel Hill. (Raleigh NC: Syme & Hall, Printers to the Convention, 1861).

Ordnances and Resolutions Passed by the State Convention of North Carolina. First Session in May and June, 1861. No. 1: An Ordnance to Dissolve the Union between the State of North Carolina and the Other States United with Her Under the Compact of Government Entitled the Constitution of the United States. (Raleigh, NC: John W. Syme, Printer to the Convention, 1862), 3. Original held at University of North Carolina Library, Call No. VC342.2 1862o, Chapel Hill, NC.

United States Census 1860 and 1860 Slave Schedules. Microfilm Publication M563, National Archives & Records Administration, Washington, DC, n.d.

United States War Department. The War of the Rebellion: A Compilation of the Official Records of the Union and Confederate Armies. Series 1-4. (Washington, DC: US War Department Printing, 1894).

Unpublished Thesis and Dissertations

Raymond Heath, Jr. "The North Carolina Militia on the Eve of Civil War." (Master's thesis, University of North Carolina, Chapel Hill, North Carolina, 1974).

BIBLIOGRAPHY

Richard W. Iobst, "North Carolina Mobilizes: Nine Crucial Months, December 1860-August 1861." Doctoral Dissertation, 1968, Southern Historical Collection, Wilson Library, University of North Carolina at Chapel Hill.

Roy S. Raby. "The Fayetteville Independent Light Infantry: Citizen Soldiers of Cumberland County 1793-1997." (Masters' thesis, Fayetteville State University, Fayetteville, NC, 1997).

NOTES

Chapter One

1. "Daniel R. Goodloe (Daniel Reaves), 1814-1902 Inquiry into the Causes Which Have Retarded the Accumulation of Wealth and Increase of Population in the Southern States: in Which the Question of Slavery is Considered in a Politico-Economical Point of View. By a Carolinian," *Documenting the American South*, University of North Carolina Chapel Hill. http://docsouth.unc.edu/nc/goodloe.

2. North Carolina General Assembly, "Slaves and Free Persons of Color. An Act Concerning Slaves and Free Persons of Color," North Carolina Revised Code No. 105, 1855, *Civil War Era NC*, accessed August 15, 2021, https://cwnc.omeka.chass.ncsu.edu.

3. "Republican Party Platform of 1856, June 18,1856," *The American Presidency Project*, The University of California, Santa Barbara, http://www.presidency.ucsb.edu.

4. Ibid., "The Democratic Party Platform, June 2, 1856; Guion G. Johnson. *Antebellum North Carolina: A Social History.* (Chapel Hill, NC: University of North Carolina Press, 1937), 119-121, 134.

5. "Highly Important Decision," *Raleigh Standard*, March 11, 1857, Secession Era Editorials Project, http://history.furman.edu.

6. "The Outbreak at Harper's Ferry." *Wilmington Journal*, Oct. 21, 1859, Vol. 16(8), 2. Chroniclingamerica.loc.gov.

7. Gray, Thomas R. *Confessions of Nat Turner, the Leader of the Late Insurrection in South Hampton, Va.* Original copy in Library of Congress, Call No. F232.S7T9 (Richmond, VA: T.R. Gray, 1832).

8. *Wilmington Journal*, October 21, 1859. Vol. 16(8), 2. chroniclingamerica.loc.gov.

9. James Oakes. *Slavery and Freedom: An Interpretation of the Old South.* (New York, NY: Alfred A. Knopf, 1990), xxii, 244-254; Stampp,

Kenneth M. *The Peculiar Institution.* (New York, NY: Vintage Books, 1954), 427-435; Phillips, Ulrich B. *Life and Labor in the Old South.* (Columbia, SC: University of South Carolina Press), xix, 22-24, 217-225, 361-364; Federal Writer's Project: Slave Narrative Project, Vol. 11, North Carolina, Part 2, Jackson-Yellerday. (1936). Manuscript/Mixed Material, (Washington, DC: 1941, Library of Congress), 2-6. Https://www.loc.gov/item/mesn112/.

10   Ibid., Isabell Henderson, Wilmington, N.C., 1932 Interview.

11   *Wilmington Journal,* October 28, 1859, 2.

12   *Harriet Tubman: Antislavery Activist.* (New York, NY: Chelsea House Publishers, 2004), 68-69; McPherson, James M. *Battle Cry of Freedom.* (New York, NY: Oxford University Press, 2003), 205; Taylor, Marian.

13   "A Misnomer," Wilmington *Daily Herald,* October 26, 1859, *Secession Era Editorials Project,* http://history.furman.edu.

14   Tolbert, Noble. (Ed). *The Papers of John W. Ellis,* Vol. 1, (Raleigh, NC: Department of Archives and History, 1964), 333. (Hereafter Tolbert), Letter of John Ellis to John Floyd, December 10, 1859, *Civil War Era NC,* accessed August 14, 2021, https://cwnc.omeka.chass.ncsu.edu/items/show/761. Floyd was later accused of covertly removing 250,000 arms from Federal arsenals and sending them to Southern armories in 1859, (see later chapter A Series of Ironic Events) although there is no evidence Ellis was involved in any improprieties with Floyd.

15   Letter from Zebulon B. Vance to William Dickson, December 11, 1860, quoted in "North Carolinians Debate Secession," *North Carolina Digital History.* www.learnnc.org/lp/editions/nchist-civilwar/4589.

16   Craven County December 1860 resolutions, *North Carolina Digital Collections,* http://digital.ncdcr.gov. (Hereafter NC Digital Archive)

17   Ibid.

18   Tolbert, Joseph Todd to John Ellis, Boone, December 15, 1859.

NOTES

19 John Willis Ellis Papers, 1844-1958. #242 Southern Historical Collection, Coll No. 00242, Official Papers and Correspondence, 1861, pertaining particularly to Secession and the beginning of the Civil War; Folders 10-11. Wilson Library, University of North Carolina, Chapel Hill. (Hereafter Ellis Papers)

20 Lincoln, Abraham. Abraham Lincoln papers: Series 1. General Correspondence. 1833 to 1916. ID No. MSS30189. Winfield Scott to Abraham Lincoln, recalling his communication with President James Buchanan of Dec. 15, 1861. Report on Southern Forts. Manuscript-Fixed Material. www.loc.gov/itemma10850000/. (Hereafter Lincoln Papers)

21 Ibid.

22 Ibid.

23 Ibid.

24 Cape Fear Historical Institute. www.cfhi.net.

25 John Willis Ellis Diary, Transcript. Entries for November 28 & 29, 1860. In J.W. Ellis Papers, 1844-1958. #242 Southern Historical Collection, Coll No. 00242, Official Papers and Correspondence, 1861, Folder 25. Wilson Library, University of North Carolina, Chapel Hill. (Hereafter Ellis Diary)

26 Cape Fear Historical Institute. www.cfhi.net.

27 *The Congressional Globe*. The Official Proceedings of Congress. Vol. 30, Senate, 36th Congress, Thursday December, 6, 1860. (Washington, D.C., John C. Reeves, Pub. 1860). 113-116. See also: «The Hedgehog and the Foxes,» *Journal of the Abraham Lincoln Association*, Vol. 12(1), (1991), 49-65; McPherson, James M. *Abraham Lincoln and the Second American Revolution*, (New York, NY: Oxford University Press, 1991), 113-130.

28 Lincoln Papers, Winfield Scott to Abraham Lincoln, March 10, 1861.

29 Ibid.

Chapter Two

30 William S. Powell. *Dictionary of North Carolina Biography*, Vol. 2., D-G. (Chapel Hill, North Carolina: UNC Press, 1996), 151-152. (Hereafter Powell) See also: James S. Brawley. *The Rowan Story 1753-1953: A Narrative History of Rowan County, North Carolina.* (Salisbury, North Carolina: Rowan Printing, 1953); John W. Ells Papers, NC Dept of Archives and History; John W. Ellis Collection, Southern Historical Collection, Wilson Library, University of North Carolina at Chapel Hill.

31 *Fayetteville Observer*, Secession Flag At Wilmington, January 7, 1861, *Civil War Era NC*, https://cwnc.omeka.chass.ncsu.edu.

32 "General Assembly Resolutions submitted and referred to committee", January 1861. "...Resolutions submitted and referred to committee", *NC General Assembly*, 1861. January 7, 1861, Vol. 33, 1-7. North Carolina State Archives.

33 Clayton E. Jewett and John O. Allen. *Slavery in the South: A State-by-State History.* (Westport, Connecticut: Greenwood Press, 2004), 192.

34 James Sprunt, *Chronicles of the Cape Fear River: 1600-1916.* (Spartanburg, SC, 1974; reprint, Wilmington, NC: Broadfoot Publishing, 1992), 276-280. (Hereafter Sprunt)

35 Ethel Herring and Carole Williams. *Fort Caswell in War and Peace.* (Wendell, NC: Broadfoot Publishing, 1983), 25-54. (Hereafter Herring and Williams, 1983); See also Herring and Williams, *Fort Caswell in War and Peace.* (Wendell, NC: Broadfoot Publishing, Revised edition, 1999), 10. (Hereafter Herring and Williams, 1999); Walter Clark, (Ed.), *Histories of the Several Regiments and Battalions from North Carolina in the Great War 1861-1865, Written by Members of the Various Commands.* (Raleigh, NC:1901). Vol. 5; 24. (Hereafter Clark).

36 Herring and Williams, 1999, 18.

37 Wilson Angley, "*A History of Fort Johnston on the Lower Cape Fear,*" (Southport, NC: Southport Historical Society, 1996), 68-76. (Hereafter Angley)

NOTES

38 Herring and Williams, 1999, 21-22.

39 John B. Moore, (Ed.), *The Works of James Buchanan Comprising his Speeches, State Papers, and Private Correspondence.* Vol. 11, (Philadelphia and London: J.B. Lippincott Co., 1860-1868), 100-102. (Hereafter Buchanan)

40 Ibid., 70.

41 Ibid., 80-105.

42 *Official Records of the War of the Rebellion,* Series 1, Vol. 1, 120-125; 132-136. (Hereafter OR)

43 Lincoln Papers, April 1, 1861. Winfield Scott to Abraham Lincoln.

44 *OR,* Series 1, Vol. 1, 132-136.

45 Sprunt, 268-272.

46 Herring & Williams, 22; Sprunt, 272.

47 *Wilmington Daily Herald,* January 8, 1861. Vol. 7(202), Newspaper Reading Room, SN 920739122, Library of Congress.

48 Ibid.

49 Lincoln Papers, April 1, 1860. Winfield Scott to Abraham Lincoln; *Wilmington Daily Herald,* January 8, 1861.

50 Ibid.

51 Ibid.

52 Ibid.

53 Fonvielle, Jr. Chris E. *Faces of Fort Fisher.* (Carolina Beach, NC: Slapdash Publishing, 2013), 7. (Hereafter Fonvielle, Faces of Fort Fisher)

54 OR, Series 1, Vol. 1, 120-125.

55 Sprunt, 268.

56 *Wilmington Daily Herald,* February 21, 1861. Vol. 17 (26), 1. https://chroniclingamerica.loc.gov.

57 Ibid., March 7, 1861. Vol. 17, (28), 2.

58 Philip S. Foner. *Business and Slavery: The New York Merchants and the Irrepressible Conflict.* (Chapel Hill, North Carolina: UNC Press, 1942) 273-278.

59 William D. Rawle. *A view of the Constitution of the United States of America.* (Durham, North Carolina: Carolina Academic Press, 2009), 98-121.

Chapter Three

60 Militia Act of 1792, Second Congress, Session 1. Chapter 28, Second Act, Article 1, ss. 1-5(i). Passed May 2, 1792. Printed Ephemera Collection, Portfolio 222, Folder 13, Library of Congress. (Hereafter Militia Act of 1792, Second Act) Provides for the organization and arming of the militia and required all white males between ages 18-45 to serve in the state militia; Raymond Heath, Jr. "The North Carolina Militia on the Eve of Civil War." (Master's thesis, University of North Carolina, 1974), "Antebellum Militia". (Hereafter Heath)

61 Stephen Bradley, *North Carolina Militia Officers Roster as Contained in the Adjutant General's Officers Roster.* (Wilmington, NC: Broadfoot Publishing, 1992), 1. (Hereafter Bradley)

62 Governor's Office Record Book, Vol. 5, 1841- 1855, No.1349. Cited in *Abstracts of Letters of Resignation of Militia Officers in North Carolina 1779-1840.* Compiled and abstracted by Tim Kearney. (Raleigh, NC: Walsworth Printing Company, 1992), iv-xiii. (Hereafter Kearney)

63 James S. Brawley, *Rowan County: A Brief History.* (Raleigh, NC: NC Department of Archives and History, 1974), 57. (Hereafter Brawley)

64 Bradley, vi.

65 Brawley, 55.

66 Clark, Vol 1., 4-5, Vol. 2, 16; Wilmington Light Infantry Papers, (W.L.I.) 1853-1953. North Carolina Room, New Hanover County Public Library, Wilmington, North Carolina. (Hereafter WLI papers)

NOTES

67 Blades, Thomas E. & Wike, John E. Career of a Flag. *The North Carolina Historical Review,* Vol. 26(4), 439-445. This article states that Edward Cantwell's younger siblings, Colonel John L. Cantwell was once a member of the Rowan Rifle Guards, who garrisoned Fort Caswell and Fort Johnston in April-July 1861, although his name does not appear on later muster rolls for Company K, 4th NCST.

68 Ibid.

69 Ibid.

70 Ibid.

71 Ibid.

72 Roy S. Raby, S. "The Fayetteville Independent Light Infantry: Citizen Soldiers of Cumberland County 1793-1997." (Masters' thesis, Fayetteville State University, 1997), 23.

Chapter Four

73 John Lucas Paul Cantwell Papers 1830-1925. Collection No. 03027, Southern Historical Collection, Wilson Library, University of North Carolina at Chapel Hill. (Hereafter Cantwell Papers)

74 Ibid.

75 Ibid.

76 Ibid.

77 OR, Ser. 1, Vol. 51(3), (1891); 6.

78 Clark, Vol.5, 24.

79 Ibid.

80 OR, Series 1, Vol. 1, (1888); 476. Note that Reilly's report is dated January 9, 1861, but other original documents show the militia captured Fort Caswell on January 10, 1861, including Colonel John Cantwell's account in Clark, Vol. 5 cited above.

81 Ibid., 476.

82 Clark, Vol. 5, 24.

83 Ibid., 25.

84 *Wilmington Journal*, Vol. 17(23), January 31, 1861, 1; Gov. John W. Ellis Papers, Box No. G. P. 150, Correspondence, 1861: January 1861. Manuscript Collection, NC State Archives. (Hereafter Ellis Papers)

85 Tolbert, Noble J. (Ed.). *The Papers of John Willis Ellis*. Vol. 2. (Raleigh, NC: NC State Archives, 1964), 563. (Hereafter Tolbert)

86 Lincoln, Abraham. Abraham Lincoln Papers: Series 2. General Correspondence 1858-1864. Abraham to Horace Greeley. Clipping from the Friday, Aug. 23, 1862, *Daily National Intelligencer*, Washington, D.C. Library of Congress. (Hereafter Lincoln Papers)

87 *Wilmington Journal*, Vol. 17(23), January 31, 1861, 1.

88 Ibid., 555; OR, Series 1, Vol. 3, (1889); 39.

89 Angley, 70.

90 *Wilmington Journal*, January 17, 1861. Vol. 17, (21), 2. https://chroniclingamerica.loc.gov.

91 Tolbert, Vol. 2, 553. See also OR, Series 1, Vol. 1, (1901), 474.

92 *Wilmington Journal*, Vol. 17(23), January 31, 1861, 1. https://chroniclingamerica.loc.gov.

93 Ibid.

94 Ellis Papers, January -February 1861.

95 Ibid.

96 Ibid., January 17, 1861, 2.

Chapter Five

97 OR, Series 1, Vol. 3, 39; Tolbert, Vol. 2, 257.

98 Randall Osborne & Jeffrey C. Weaver, *The Virginia State Rangers and Virginia State Line*, (Lynchburg, VA: H.E. Howard, 1994), 23-24, 114-121; (Hereafter Osborne and Weaver) Swanberg, W.A. "Was the Secretary of War a Traitor?" (Feb. 1963), *American Heritage*, Vol. 14(2), 11-18.). (Hereafter Swanberg). John B. Floyd was later promoted to Brigadier General and commanded the Virginia State Line in 1862-1863, and a battalion of infantry in 1864. His

NOTES

tenure as general officer was similarly wrought with allegations of fraud and mismanagement of public funds, as he was accused of pilfering thousands of dollars, he received intended to purchase equipment for his troops that was never accounted for.

99   Militia Act of 1792, Second Act.

100 Swanberg 13-18; OR, Series 1, Vol. 3, 39.

101 Ibid; Osborne and Weaver, 114-121.

102 Tolbert, Vol. 2, 257; *North Carolina Convention & Military Board (1861-1862)*. Original held at North Carolina Collection, Call No. VC342.2 1861d Vol. 1, University of North Carolina at Chapel Hill. (Raleigh NC: Syme & Hall, Printers to the Convention, 1861), 30-31. (Hereafter NC Convention & Military Board, 1861-1862.

103 Swanberg, 16-18, Osborne and Weaver, 23-24.

104 *Carolina Watchman*, January 30, 1861. Salisbury, NC: Rowan County Public Library, Microfilm held in The Edith M. Clark History Room. (Hereafter *Carolina Watchman*) See also: *The Carolina Watchman*, Index by James Brawley, Rowan County Library, Salisbury, NC, 166. (Hereafter Brawley's Index)

105 Ibid., March 5, 1861.

106 Ibid.

107 Ibid., March 19, 1861; Bacot, Ada White. A Confederate Nurse: The Diary of Ada W. Bacot, 1860-1863. (Columbia, SC: University of South Carolina Press, 1994), 27.

108 Clark, Vol. 1, 231; Vol. 2, 435.

109 Ibid.

110 Stephen Bradley, North Carolina Militia Officers Roster as Contained in the Adjutant General's Officers Roster. (Wilmington, NC: Broadfoot Publishing, 1992), 2-7. (Hereafter Bradley)

111 "The Forts at the South." Fayetteville Observer, April 4, 1861. Vol. 10(1010), 3. *Civil War Era NC*, accessed August 14, 2021, https://cwnc.omeka.chass.ncsu.edu.

Chapter Six

112 *Carolina Watchman*, April 23, 1861.113   OR Series 1, Vol. 51(3), (1891), 12.

114 Louis H. Manarin and Weymouth T. Jordan Jr., North Carolina Troops, 1861-1865: A Roster, Vol. 6, 267, and Vol. 10, 218. Also, Angley, 23-24, and Herring and Williams, 1999, 24. (Hereafter Manarin and Jordan)

115 Clark, Vol. 5, 27.

116 Ibid.

117 Herring and Williams, 1999, 24.

118 John A. Stikeleather, Recollections of the Civil War in the United States 1861-1865. (Olin, N.C.: 27 May 1909. University of North Carolina Chapel Hill, Southern Historical Collection), 2. (Hereafter Stikeleather)

119 *Statesville Landmark*, June 6, 1911.

120 *Carolina Watchman*, April 16, 1861.

121 *Carolina Watchman, April 21, 1861.*

122 Ibid.; Brawley, 91; Compiled Military Service Records, Group 109, National Archives, Washington DC. Microfilm, Rowan County Library, Roll 140, Capt. Francis McNeely (Hereafter CMSR); Manarin and Jordan, Vol. 6, 446.

123 *Carolina Watchman* May 9, 1861.

124 Stikeleather, 3.

125 *Salisbury Banner*, April 23, 1861.

126 Elle M. Andrews, *Elle's Book, Being the Journal Kept by Elle M. Andrews from April 23, 1861, through May 1865.* Transcribed and annotated by Ann Campbell. Elle Andrews was from Statesville, NC, and was the sister of Captain John Barr Andrews, who commanded the Iredell Blues. The Iredell Blues served in the garrison at Fort Caswell and Fort Johnston and later became Company A, 4th NCST.

NOTES

Chapter Seven

127 Tolbert, Vol. 2, 775; John Lucas Paul Cantwell Papers 1830-1925. Collection No. 03027, Southern Historical Collection, Wilson Library, University of North Carolina at Chapel Hill.

128 Richard W. Iobst, "North Carolina Mobilizes: Nine Crucial Months, December 1860-August 1861." Doctoral Dissertation, University of North Carolina at Chapel Hill, 1968, 38-39.

129 Letter from Pvt. George Deal, Cabarrus Guards, May 25, 1861, to Miss Catie Sloop of Rowan County. Original held in private collection of George Patterson, Concord, NC. Used with permission.

130 James Lilly, Letter to Ms. Catie, from Fort Caswell, May 4, 1861. Private Collections, Miscellaneous Papers, 1689-1912, Lilly Family Papers, 1785-1863. NC State Archives. (Hereafter Lilly)

131 Ibid.

132 Ibid.

133 Ibid.

134 *North Carolina Convention & Military Board 1861-1862*, 1-3; 30-31.

135 Brown, 3-4.

136 Brawley, 93.

137 *Carolina Watchman*, May 1, 1861.

138 Fred C. Foard, Civil War Remembrances. NC Archives, Private Manuscript Collection, 11-12.

139 Stikeleather, 2-3.

140 *Wilmington Daily Herald*, 18 July 1861.

141 *Carolina Watchman*, May 2, 1861.

142 Ibid., May 10, 1861.

143 *Carolina Watchman*, May 20, 1861: Letter reprinted from the May 18, 1861 *Charleston Courier*.

144 Ibid.; *Compiled Service Records, Record Group 94, M270, Roll 136, U.S. National Archives, Washington, DC (Hereafter CSR); See also:* Civil War

Collection: Regimental Records, Muster Rolls of North Carolina State Troops 1861-1865, Co. K, 4th NCT. AG-16, Box 48, December 31, 1861. NC State Archives. Company K, 4th NCT Muster rolls in 1861 do not contain the names Reaves or Pearson; however, there was a Michael Davis who on muster rolls from 1864. Davis may have been an original member of the company as his muster date is shown only as 1861.

145 *Ordnances and Resolutions Passed by the State Convention of North Carolina. First Session in May and June 1861.* No. 1: An Ordnance to Dissolve the Union between the State of North Carolina and the Other States United with Her Under the Compact of Government Entitled the Constitution of the United States. (Raleigh, NC: John W. Syme, Printer to the Convention, 1862), 3. Original held at University of North Carolina Library, Call No. VC342.2 1862o, Chapel Hill, NC.

146 *Carolina Watchman,* May 23, 1861.

Chapter Eight

147 NC Convention, Vol. 1, Letter from Warren Winslow to Weldon Edwards, May 24, 1861, cited in the *North Carolina Convention & Military Board, 1861-1862,* 13.

148 Ibid.

149 Ibid.

150 Ibid.

151 CMSR, Roll 140, Captain F. McNeeley; *NC Convention,* 1861, 30-31.

152 Brawley, 93.

153 Ibid., 168-169; CMSR, Company K, 4th NCT; 1860 U.S. Census, Rowan County, NC, Slave Schedules; http://www.civil-war.net/pages/ordinances_secession.asp. Out of 630,000 whites who lived in North Carolina in 1860, 27,000 owned slaves; only four North Carolinians owned more than 300 slaves. In the western part of the state, there were few slaves, and unionist sentiment was much stronger than on the eastern coast and Piedmont region.

NOTES

154 Ibid., CMSR, Roll 140, McNeeley.

155 James Isaac Metts Papers, 1843-1921. Coll. No. 03624-Z, Southern Historical Papers, Wilson Library, Chapel Hill, NC. James I. Metts attended U.N.C. during the school year 1860-1861 and was interrupted when he joined the WRG in April 1861, and he later received an A.B. degree along with many other Confederate veterans whose education was halted because of the war. Metts enlisted in the 3rd NCT in April 1862 and was captured during the Gettysburg Campaign, and sent to Johnson's Island, Ohio. He rejoined his regiment in December 1864 and served until the end of the war.

156 Powell, 165.

157 Clark, Vol. 5, 28.

NAME INDEX

Anderson, Robert 20, 24, 33

Arnold, Benedict 32

Beecher, Henry Ward 10

Bowers, James 83

Boyd, William K. XIX

Brown, John 5, 6, 8, 9, 10, 12, 13, 14

Brown, Williams 102

Brunner, John 73, 83

Buchanan, James XX, XXI, 3, 4, 5, 14, 20, 22, 23, 32, 33, 34, 35, 36, 63, 65, 66, 70, 71, 79

Burr, Aaron 32

Calder, Robert E. 60

Calder, William 60

Cameron, Simon 77

Cantwell, Edward P. Chrysostom 48, 49

Cantwell, John Lucas Paul 49, 55, 56, 57, 58, 60, 62, 66, 67, 79, 80, 108, 111, 114

Cornehlson, C. 79

Cowan, John 55

Crumpler, T.N. 28

Darlingkiller, Frederick 58, 80

Davis, George 38, 39

Deal, George 90

DeRossett, W.L. 79

Dickson, William 16

Douglass, Frederick 10

Edwards, Weldon N. 106

Ellis, John W. XXI, 14, 16, 17, 18, 21, 25, 26, 28, 33, 35, 60, 63, 65, 66, 67, 68, 69, 70, 71, 73, 75, 77, 79, 80, 82, 89, 105, 107, 108, 113

Floyd, John B. 5, 14, 20, 22, 35, 69, 70, 71, 72, 80

Fremont, John C. 3

Gist, William H. 18

Goodloe, Daniel Reaves 1

Grant, Ulysses S. 56, 72

Greeley, Horace 10, 30, 36

Hardee, William 39

Hedrick, John J. 57, 58, 59, 60, 62, 79

Henderson, Isabell 9

Hoke, John F. 105, 107, 108

Holt, John 22, 24, 65

Jackson, John H. 8

Jackson, Thomas "Stonewall" 79

Jefferson, Thomas 40

Johnston, Gabriel 32

Jones, Charles R. 49

Jones, J.B. 87, 95, 100, 101

Jones, J.P. 95, 101

Lafayette, Marquis de 49

Lilly, James 90

Lincoln, Abraham XX, XXI, XXII, 1, 14, 16, 17, 18, 30, 32, 33, 36, 37, 39, 50, 56, 68, 70, 74, 77, 80, 81, 82, 84, 95, 96, 101

Long, H.C. 103

McNeely, Francis 83, 96, 103, 108

Meares, John 22, 79

Metts, James I. 112

Metts, William Penn 52

Moore, A.B. 25

Moore, B.R. 93

Pearson, Richard M. 25

Pickens, Francis 33

Rawle, William 40

Reilly, James S. 57, 80, 92

Scott, Winfield 19, 20, 21, 22, 23, 34, 36, 37, 49

Seward, William 37, 38

Sloop, Catie 90

Smith, Gerritt 10

Stevenson, James M. 79

Stikeleather, John 97

Thurston, Stephen D. 57, 60, 61, 62

Todd, Joseph 16

Tubman, Harriet 10

Turner, Alfred 106

Turner, J. Mc L. 95

Vance, Zebulon Baird 15

Vollers, Hanke 47

Winslow, Warren 106, 107

ABOUT THE AUTHOR

Dr. Philip Hatfield holds a bachelor's degree in psychology and history, two master's degrees in psychology, and a doctorate in Clinical Psychology. He is a veteran of the U.S. Air Force and a member of the Company of Military Historians. Dr. Hatfield has written six books and numerous scholarly articles on the Civil War.

35th Star Publishing
Charleston, West Virginia
www.35thstar.com

www.ingramcontent.com/pod-product-compliance
Lightning Source LLC
Chambersburg PA
CBHW030039100526
44590CB00011B/261